ALONG THE SOUTH WEST WAY

ALONG THE SOUTH WEST WAY

Part 1
MINEHEAD TO BUDE

A. G. COLLINGS

TABB HOUSE
Padstow, Cornwall.

First published 1985
by Tabb House, 11 Church Street, Padstow, Cornwall.

Copyright © A. G. Collings 1985
ISBN 0907018 28 9 Limp
ISBN 0907018 46 7 Cased

Printed in Great Britain by Quintrell & Co. Ltd., Wadebridge, Cornwall.

CONTENTS

The author offers a choice of route along several stretches of the way; the descriptions of short alternatives are printed in small type size with wide margins.

SKETCH MAPS AND GRID REFERENCES

ACKNOWLEDGEMENTS

NO ONE can write a detailed guide to a 560 mile walk without being under an obligation to a large number of people. The problem is to remember them all.

My principal debt is to the staff of Devon Library Services at Exeter, in particular to the Westcountry Studies Library, but also to the Reference and Lending Departments.

I am also grateful for being allowed access to the libraries of the University of Exeter, the North Devon Athenaeum, and the Royal Institution of Cornwall.

I have also to express my gratitude to Mr G. J. Paley, of the Devon and Exeter Institution, for placing his unrivalled knowledge of the sources of Devon history so generously at my disposal; and to Philip Carter, Secretary of the South West Way Association, for advice and encouragement over the last few years.

Others who have searched through their records on my behalf are Duncan Mackay, Deputy Secretary of the Open Spaces Society; Paul Kershaw, Law Librarian at the University of Exeter; John Longhurst, until recently Honorary Curator of the Ilfracombe Museum; and Mr J. M. Rowe, Head Librarian of the North Devon Athenaeum, who also kindly provided me with a copy of the James Braund broadsheet.

My thanks also to the editors of *The Times*, the *Western Morning News*, and the *Cornishman*, for allowing me to quote extracts from their papers.

Finally it has to be said that the interpretation of the facts provided remains solely my own.

A. G. Collings

HOW THE WEST WAS LOST —
AN UNOFFICIAL HISTORY

THE right of an Englishman to walk the bounds of his native land does not appear to have any basis in law, although in earlier times such a right was widely believed to exist. It was a belief particularly common among the indigenous landowners in the South West, and may perhaps have its roots in the Middle Ages when the coastal landowners would have been forced to tolerate the entire parish tramping over their property during the Rogationtide ceremony of perambulating the parish bounds. But this tolerance certainly extended into Victorian times, which meant that a rambler who set out to to follow the coastguard track a hundred years ago would find virtually nothing to bar his progress.

Doubt was then cast on the issue of access to the cliffs by Sir Frederick Pollock, the Oxford professor of jurisprudence and a noted walker. He looked into the question for a book he was writing on the land laws, but was forced to admit that he had been unable to discover any legal authority for the belief, although my own understanding is that even today the law upholds the right of the parish officials (vicar, churchwardens and sidesmen) to go onto private property to perform the long obsolete perambulation ceremony.

The gradual replacement of the traditional landowners by incomers with radically different views of their obligations to the wider public led to disputes over access, some of which were referred to the courts. One such dispute was at a time when the judiciary was taking a more hostile view of rights of way than it ever did before or since, with the result that an adverse legal precedent was established and this led to substantial stretches of the coast being denied to the walker.

It is therefore ironic that the first of four Government reports within a decade to recommend the re-opening of the coastguard path should have been from a committee chaired by a Lord Chief Justice, and that the response of Government should have been less than enthusiastic.

But to go back to the beginning, the earliest visitor to the south west coastline was Mesolithic man, who arrived in this country before the first farmers and therefore did not need anyone's permission. He was dependent for subsistence in winter on the limpets and mussels that he found upon the rocky shores, and may also have collected laver. The practice has continued whenever times were hard, even up to the present century. It is known in West Cornwall as 'going trigging'.

Almost as vital to Mesolithic man would have been the search for flint pebbles, from which were produced the arrow-tips and scrapers needed for summer hunting expeditions inland, principally for deer. There are few parts of the south-west coast where the flint flakes discarded by these hunter-gatherers have not been found.

The next specifically coastal activity was fishing, and the Middle Ages saw the establishment of fishing communities all round the coast, and no doubt paths to the nearest sandy shores where boats could be beached in rough weather. Such paths may even have connected neighbouring villages, but with the inevitable rivalry between communities fishing the same stretch of God's ocean, social visitors must have been not only few, but uncertain of their reception.

By the eighteenth century the increasing needs of the Government for more revenue led to widespread imposition of customs duties, and hence to the diversification of the fishing communities into a related activity, smuggling, that was eventually to lead to a complete coastal path, although initially it could only have discouraged tourists. It was an early tourist, Daniel Defoe, who observed in 1724 that 'smuggling and roguing . . . is the reigning commerce of all this part of the English coast, from the mouth of the Thames to Land's End'.

Twelve years later Parliament responded by passing the first of several Draconian acts aimed at suppressing the evil, whereby 'any person or persons lurking, waiting, or loitering within five miles from the sea-coast . . . if such persons shall not give satisfactory account of themselves, and their callings and employments . . . shall be committed to the house of correction, there to be whipt and kept to hard labour for any time . . . not exceeding one month.'[1]

It may be helpful here to reassure those of a nervous disposition that the Act was repealed in 1825. Although it has not been part of

English law for over 150 years the attitude it engendered, among officialdom, towards the coastal loiterer can seem on occasion to have survived into the present day.

A further factor militating against the early establishment of a tourist industry was the way coastal scenery was perceived at this time. During the eighteenth century there was very much a vogue for classifying scenery. Three categories were recognised; the beautiful, or that which appealed to the aesthetic sense; the sublime, or that which induced exaltation and fear; and, most controversial and difficult to understand today, the picturesque.

This last category derives from the Italian *pittoresco*, meaning that which makes up a picture, in other words the rules of composition familiar to anyone who has ever opened a book on landscape painting or photography; foreground, middle ground, background, and sidescreens. There was room for argument over what constituted the ideal foreground, with some prescribing a certain roughness; hence the purpose-built 'ruins' in gentlemen's parks and goats being regarded as more picturesque than sheep. It was the Reverend William Gilpin, widely regarded as the Master of the Picturesque, who suggested in his work on the Lake District that a group of banditti would make an appropriate foreground, while another authority suggested that the coastal scene should be adorned by smugglers.

The most extreme critic of coastal scenery at this time seems to have been the Reverend Richard Warner, who had been Gilpin's curate for seven years and presumably understood the rules. After his equestrian tour of Cornwall in August 1808, which took in not only Land's End and the Lizard, but also Tintagel and Bude, he wrote 'it can offer no claim to the praise of the picturesque or beautiful'. This only left the sublime; in other words the scenery inspired a sense of awe in the beholders. Nor was this an isolated view. A study of the prints of the period shows that almost all of them tend to exaggerate both the height and steepness of the cliffs.

But things were beginning to change. In 1811 J. M. W. Turner first visited Devon and Cornwall to make the series of sketches that were to be published in 1826 as *Picturesque Views on the Southern Coast of England*, perhaps the first artist to depict the coastal scenery as it actually was. In contrast William Daniell at the end of his *Voyage Round Great Britain* in 1825 was still giving his imagination a free hand.

Meanwhile, the Draconian legislation had signally failed to deter the smugglers. Duties on spirits were so high and the economies of scale were such that on the Kent and Sussex coast smuggling was really big business. Profits on a successful run were so great that it paid the organisers to assemble up to two hundred farm labourers (and pay them for a single night as much as they would earn in a week), half of them to carry the goods inland and the other half, armed to the teeth, to prevent anyone interfering. It was indeed a case of 'Watch the wall, my darling, while the Gentlemen go by!'

Clearly no government could tolerate such widespread lawlessness. The initial response was to establish the Preventive Water Guard in 1809, followed by a coast blockade of Kent and Sussex a few years later. This latter involved a night patrol by sailors along the shore, described by a writer in the *United Services Journal* for 1839. 'Moreover, the fatigue and loneliness of trudging six or seven hours of a winter's night along solitary cliffs, dreary sand-hills, and ever-lasting shingles, with the unintermitting watchfulness required to avoid falling over precipices, or stumbling into ambuscades of armed smugglers, soon made seamen tired of "soldiering" as they called it . . .'

But however unpopular it was with the seamen, it had attractions for people in high places. During a debate on smuggling in the House of Commons in April 1821 a Wiltshire MP assured the House that 'the coast of Devon and Dorset were in a state quite as disturbed as the coast of Sussex'. Although this could hardly have been the case, in the event Parliament decided to extend the system to the entire coast of the British Isles, and from January 1822 the Coastguard service was born, and, as a consequence, the South West Way.

The idea was to throw a human cordon around the entire coastline, which required the creation of a coastal footpath for them to patrol. The concentration of manpower varied with the distance from the French coast; along the Kent coast there was one coastguard to every hundred yards, while in South Devon the figure was between a quarter and half a mile. The difficulties for the smugglers in rounding Land's End meant that the Bristol

Channel coast could be much less well guarded, with each man being required to patrol two or three miles.

The years of depression following the Napoleonic Wars meant that there was no shortage of disciplined ex-servicemen able to tolerate the rigours of one of the most demanding jobs ever. Long experience of the ease with which Customs officers could be bribed led to stringent regulations covering the conduct of the coastguard. To prevent collusion, none were allowed to serve within twenty miles of their birth-place, while 'any individual intermarrying with the family of a reputed or notorious smuggler, or lodging in his house, or contracting any improper intimacy with him, will be dismissed'. Even the suspicion of collusion could lead to dismissal.

As might well be imagined, such a group of men, whose sole function was to prevent impoverished communities from gaining access to virtually their only luxury, were detested. No one would provide them with lodgings, and it is said that landowners initially refused to provide the land on which their barrack-like stations were built.

The stations of the early period date from a time when the Government was faced with a choice between reform and revolution, and did not fancy either. With practice, the buildings, designed to stand a siege, can be recognised from a distance, even now some have been converted to holiday homes. The most characteristic features are the intercommunicating porches, which allowed the occupants to move from one end of the building to the other without exposing their persons to the wrath of a risen people. With the exception of Southern Ireland in the 1920s, such precautions proved unnecessary.

On their night patrols the men were certainly prepared for trouble. To quote one of the leading authorities on smuggling, Commander H. N. Shore (later Lord Teignmouth):

As regards arms, the patrols, when equipped for the night's duty, carried a brace of heavy pistols, a cutlass, several rounds of ammunition, and a blue-light for giving the alarm. The pistols were generally carried inside the breast of the great-coat. In some districts a musket and fixed bayonet were substituted for the cutlass, the bayonet being further secured by a lashing — details of this sort being regulated by the inspecting commanders to suit local circumstances.

Three paragraphs from the Special Instructions issued by the Admiralty as late as 1866, a time when smuggling was all but eliminated, show that even then there was to be no relaxation of the vigilance.

Officers of Stations are to be particularly cautious not to give rest to too many of the Men, under an impression that the violence of the weather, and state of the coast or beach render a landing impracticable; always bear in mind, that the smugglers wholly disregard the loss of their boats, provided they can run their goods.

Officers are not themselves to take charge of any guard, but to proceed along the coast at uncertain times, as well as after midnight and towards daylight in the morning, as in the evening or early part of the night, in order to ascertain that the Patrols are on the alert, and to give directions for an occasional change of guards; observing that the Men are not to be withdrawn from duty until after broad daylight.

Officers are frequently to visit creeks and bye places within the limits of their Station, where it is probable small craft may be concealed for the purpose of smuggling, and they are distinctly to understand that they will be held responsible for any smuggling transaction which may take place within the limits of their Station, or for the escape of any smugglers, if occasioned by negligence, want of courage, or other misconduct on their part, or if they omit to represent any such misconduct on the part of the men under their orders.

For a more personal account, Commander Shore quoted an old coastguardman:

The work was terrible. Why, Sir, in the winter months we had to be on our guards by dusk, which meant leaving home at four or half-past, and we never got back again till nearly eight next morning. The only 'nights in' we got was when our turn came round to be day watchmen at the station — once in ten days or so; and perhaps two nights before the full moon and two nights afterwards; though, even then, we seldom got more than half nights off, and if smuggling boats were expected off the coast, of course all the crew had to be out.
I've often been that done up that I could scarcely walk home, and many is the time I've gone down to the water and washed my face to keep my eyes open. Oh, it was enough to kill a horse, I can tell you; only a strong man could stand the work!

Initially pitched battles were fought with smugglers along the Kent and Sussex coasts, with fatalities on both sides, before the superior training and full-time commitment of the coastguard gained the upper hand, forcing the smugglers to resort to smaller scale, more covert methods that were traditional in the South West. In addition, the conversion of the Government to free trade led to a slashing of the tariffs between 1842 and 1853, and with it the source of the smugglers' profits, although a writer in the *United Services Journal* attributed the decline of smuggling '. . . beyond all, to the reduced price and improved quality of British spirits'.

Hence, from the 1850s there began a reduction in coastguard manpower that continues to this day despite the changed role of the service. Yet the night patrol was continued, in theory if not in practice, into the present century, and as a survival from more perilous times, at the discretion of the station commander a loaded revolver could still be carried.

Even while the smugglers were still active, the first access battle had been fought and won. In about 1838 John Ames, 'a gentleman of large fortune' and an exceptionally reactionary landowner, had acquired the Pinney estate, about a mile to the west of Lyme Regis, and built a large wall around the property, which included the coast-path. The people of the town came together, and having failed to persuade him to provide an alternative path, sought redress through the courts.

The case was heard at the Exeter Assizes, where some thirty witnesses provided evidence of usage of the path 'back as far as living memory could trace'. Of particular interest in view of subsequent events was the claim by the prosecuting counsel that twenty years usage was all that was required for the proof of a right of way.[2] Although the jury found against Ames, he spent some £10,000 in legal fees in a fruitless attempt to get the decision reversed.

It seems that from its very inception the coastguard path was potentially available to the casual walker as a recreational recourse, but in the nature of things the only first-hand evidence of such use is that provided by literary figures. One walker appears to have been years ahead of the rest of the field; Walter White, trained as a cabinet-maker but with a prodigious capacity for self-education that in the expanding economy of Victorian Britain was to lead him eventually to promotion to Assistant Secretary of the Royal Society — the senior administrative post of perhaps the most eminent intellectual body in the world at that time.

His connection with the Royal Society began in 1844 when he became library assistant, which entitled him to the month of July off. It was his practice to devote it to a pedestrian excursion either in Britain or on the Continent. In 1854 he turned his attention westward, and published the account of his travels, including some 200 miles of the south-west coast-path, in *A Londoner's Walk to the Land's End*. 'I had come to see the cliffs with all their variety of form and outline, and the glorious expanse of sea beyond ... where a coastguard could walk, I could walk also.'

It was his belief that 'an Englishman has an inherent right of way along the edge of his own country'[3] that establishes him as the first of the compulsive coast walkers, and it is very significant that having satisfied the first coastguard that he encountered that he was not a contrabandist, he refers to no other obstruction along the path.

This period must have been the 'Golden Age' of the South West Way, although there were very few who took advantage of it. But the emergence of the seaside resorts meant an increasing number of visitors, a minority of whom did not know how to behave in the countryside. This led to a number of landowners along the North Devon coast either charging for admission to the cliffs, in the belief that this would discourage undesirable elements, or even totally excluding the public.

The restrictions at Clovelly, Ilfracombe, and Lynton so incensed one walker that he was provoked to write to *The Times* on the subject in September 1871, although his resort to exaggeration can hardly have improved his case. 'Here, where I wandered years ago without let or hindrance, fished, sketched, roved about caves, corners, coves, and covers, are now spiked fences, man traps, spring guns, and every other deterrent abomination ...'

Actually the particular engines of oppression referred to had been illegal since 1827, although curiously a man trap presented by a local hotel is displayed in the museum at Lynton.

Where only a few years ago I strolled at will over gigantic crags, wave-worn rocks and precipitous hill-sides, tangled with furze, eglantine, and honeysuckle, I can only pass now through gateways, guarded fences, and at the demand of a toll ... Now what I wish to urge is a healthier tone among the owners of property which happens to be a favourite resort with the ramblers and scramblers of England, old and young. Property has its duties as well as rights, however much the 'other side' may be disposed to deny our claims. ... Will our good friends reflect that the beauties of God's nature are not all their own, that accident has given them what they possess, and that to deny their fellow creatures a peep into this loveliness is at once selfish, unbecoming, and to be resented?

This produced correspondence both for and against, one writer insisting

'I have lived on the coast of Cornwall, and have travelled much, and have never before found the headland walk otherwise than free. ... What has become of the people's invariable headland walk? Has not a sacred privilege been usurped? ... I can see nothing but niggardliness and injustice on the part of the landowners, and that shame lies at the door of the people of the district who have tolerated it'.

The Times considered the issue of sufficient importance to devote an editorial to it. On this occasion it took an elitist stance, considering the sixpenny toll exacted on both sides of Clovelly to be 'not a very extravagent imposition', and continuing with an interesting example of the semantics of the period, 'such property ... requires to be defended ... from the inroads of the noisy and unappreciative excursionists, who only make the place intolerable to the Tourist.' But the debate seems to have prevented the exclusion of the public from the cliffs from spreading beyond North Devon.

During the 1880s there was a vogue among landowners for closing footpaths. It seems to have been centred in the Lake District, where it provoked Ruskin to write to the *Pall Mall Gazette* in 1885 'of all the mean and wicked things a landlord can do, shutting up his footpath is the nastiest'. The following year Canon Rawnsley, co-founder of the National Trust, wrote in the *Contemporary Review* that twenty-two supposed ancient rights of way in the Ambleside area alone had been closed.

The nearest to the South West that the contagion appears to have reached was St Ishmaels, where part of what is now the Pembrokeshire coast path was saved by the action of the local Congregationalist minister in spearheading opposition to closure, which led to a favourable verdict at the Haverfordwest Assizes in 1887.

The 1890s must have been the end of the Golden Age of the South West Way, before judges came to take a radically different view of the rights of the pedestrian. Soon developers moved in, intent on making money from the increasing number of tourists. The walking tour was then very much the fashion among the young, particularly undergraduates on vacation and city clerks released from their office stools for a fortnight.

The quality of coastal scenery seems to have been more highly appreciated then than over the next half-century, and some of the best writing on the South West Way dates from this period, notably that of John Lloyd Warden Page, a local writer, and Sir Leslie Stephen, one of the most distinguished individuals ever to walk the path.

Sir Leslie had been an accomplished alpinist, 'fleetest of foot of the whole Alpine brotherhood', until the demands of family life led him to seek less perilous pursuits closer to home. He was also the first editor of the *Dictionary of National Biography*, and the father of Virginia Woolf.

In his essay 'In Praise of Walking' he summed up the experience of South West Way walking more exactly than anything else I have found.

Of all the walks that I have made, I can remember none more delightful than those round the south-western promontory. I have followed the coast at different times from the mouth of the Bristol Avon by the Land's End to the Isle of Wight, and I am only puzzled to decide which bay or cape is the most delightful. I only know that the most delightful was the more enjoyable when placed in its proper setting by a long walk. When you have made an early start, followed the coastguard track on the slopes above the cliffs, struggled through the gold and purple carpeting of gorse and heather on the moors, dipped down into quaint little coves with a primitive fishing village, followed by the blinding whiteness of the sands round a lonely bay, and at last emerged upon a headland where you can settle into a nook of the rocks, look down upon the glorious blue of the Atlantic waves breaking into foam on the granite, and see the distant sea-levels glimmering away till they blend imperceptibly into cloudland; then you can consume your modest sandwiches, light your pipe, and feel more virtuous and thoroughly at peace with the universe than it is easy even to conceive yourself elsewhere. I have fancied myself on such occasions to be a felicitous blend of poet and saint — which is an agreeable sensation.

Almost the only new diversion away from the coast during this period was to the west of Perranporth, where in 1885 an improvement committee had been formed with the object of encouraging tourism, to compensate for the loss of employment caused by the decline of fishing and mining. One of the achievements of the committee had been the improvement of the path out to Cligga Head, where voluntary labour was used to widen it by terracing into the hillside.

When, in 1892, the Nobel Explosives Company announced that it wished to site a dynamite factory in the area, this was welcomed by the local people as a provider of employment. What no one had foreseen was that the Explosives Acts enabled the management arbitrarily to define a danger area, and divert all rights of way outside it, with no right of appeal. Expansion of the factory a few years later led to closure of the cliff path, a decision that two of the committee who had laboured on the path refused to accept.

This led to their appearance in court charged with criminal trespass, and although the judge delayed his decision for a month, possibly to reassure himself that there was no inherent right to walk the coast that Sir Frederick Pollock had overlooked, they were both fined £1, which one of them refused to pay until threatened with imprisonment. A few months later a tourist, a lecturer at a London Technical Institute, wandered into the trap. The magistrates were unsympathetic to his claims of inadequate warning notices and that he was unaware that his Ward's *Thorough Guide* was out of date; he too was fined £1.

With the new century, an event occurred at Stonehenge that was to have the most profound consequences for the public footpath network in this country. On the last day of 1900 one of the upright stones together with its lintel fell to the ground, and in a sense the reverberations have not yet died away. Although the leading authority on the monument, Professor Flinders Petrie, took the view that no rapid injury could be done by visitors it has to be said that this was a minority view, since the habit had grown up over the previous thirty years among a small number of visitors of bringing along a hammer and chisel in order to obtain a souvenir of their visit.

The majority view was put by a committee formed from three learned bodies, including the Wiltshire Archaeological and Natural History Society, which recommended a number of measures to the landowner, Sir Edmund Antrobus, including the erection of a wire fence around the monument. Sir Edmund agreed to these measures, and proceeded to charge one shilling for admission, a move which brought him into immediate conflict with the Commons Preservation Society, which insisted that the public had acquired by immemorial usage a right of access to the monument, and that the fence was an illegal obstruction.

The dispute dragged on for four years, with the Chairman of the Commons Society quoting the previous Chancellor of the Exchequer to the effect that Sir Edmund had offered Stonehenge to the State for a grossly exorbitant sum, accompanied by the threat to sell it to an American millionaire for shipment across the Atlantic.[4] As Sir Edmund refused to give way, and was supported in his stance by Wiltshire County Council on which he sat as an Alderman, the Commons Society was forced to seek redress through the courts.

The case was heard in the Court of Chancery in April 1905 before Mr Justice Farwell, who is remembered today, if at all, as the author of the Taff Vale judgement of 1901. In this case he took the view that Trade Unions were required to compensate employers for damages inflicted on them during strikes, which rather defeated the object of the exercise. It so completely hamstrung the Unions, and silenced those members who believed that they should keep out of politics, that the Labour Representation Committee, forerunner of the present-day Labour Party, was formed to press for the law to be changed.

Having done as much as anyone this century to change the course of British politics, the learned judge was then able to turn his attention to the future of recreational rights of way. His father had been an agent to the Duke of Cleveland, the third largest landowner in England, and he himself was that very year to acquire a fifty-acre Exmoor estate, and become a life-member of the Somerset Archaeological and Natural History Society.

In this particular case Mr Justice Farwell quoted as his authority a case from 1891, involving the right to fish on the Thames at Mapledurham, in which Lord Bowen had stated in the Court of Appeal 'however continuous, however lengthy the indulgence may have been, a jury ought to be warned against extracting out of it an inference unfavourable to the person who has granted the indulgence'.[5]

Now this doctrine was to be extended to its absolute limit. Previously it had been accepted that evidence of long- continued usage of a path meant that dedication of a right of way had been made. In this case, and in the absence of documentary evidence of dedication, the learned judge ruled that unrestricted public access over a period of 5,000 years only proved a long history of indulgences which Sir Edmund was within his rights to rescind.

Mr Justice Farwell went on to expound his opinion on the subject of rights of way. 'A public road is *prima facie* a road that leads from one public place to another public place ... there cannot *prime facie* be a right for the public to go to a place where the public have no right to be. ... The action accordingly fails and ought never to have been brought.'[6] He went on to award costs of £4,000 against the Commons Preservation Society, thus nearly bankrupting the only body fighting for the right of an Englishman to stand on his native heath.

For a less one-sided view one can best turn to *The Times* leader.

It is beyond question that as far back as memory will run there has been absolutely free and uninterrupted access to Stonehenge along definite tracks, and that it has been the usual practice of visitors to approach the stones by one route and to leave by another. Mr Justice Farwell has held that this immemorial practice does not establish a legal right of way to and from Stonehenge, but merely continued permission from the owner of the soil to visit the monument.

... It would even seem to follow that there can be no access as of right to and from the sea-shore, except to a definite public landing-place, since we know that the sea-shore itself is not in the strict sense of the words a public place. ...

The idea underlying these negations of public rights seems to be that there can be no right of way except for purposes of so-called necessity — in other words, for business purposes; a right of way for purposes of pleasure or of intellectual interest the law deems impossible. . . . it is to be hoped that the question may not be allowed to rest until a higher Court has pronounced upon it.[7]

Such a hope was not to be realised in the short term. As a contemporary judge Mr Justice Sturges observed, although not until the close of his legal career, 'Justice is open to everybody, in the same way as the Ritz Hotel'.[8] The fact of the matter was that no group representing walkers' interests was sufficiently well-heeled to be able to take the case to the Appeal Court.

The Commons Preservation Society chose instead to seek to get the law changed, and drafted a Bill whereby twenty years usage of a path over land in full ownership, and forty years usage over land in family settlement would be sufficient to establish a right of way. The problem in the latter case was that the law looked on the possessor as merely a tenant without the power to dedicate a right of way. But the society, with the example before them of James Brice's Access to Mountains Bill first introduced in 1884 and no nearer the statute-book, had no reason to expect rapid results.

Just four months after the Stonehenge case, the Court of Chancery was the scene of a further reverse for the access movement, this time involving the South West Way. In 1903 a Lutheran merchant, Louis Wilhelm Ferdinand Behrens had bought land at Prussia Cove with the intention of building a house for his retirement. He immediately antagonised the local community by building a wall around his property thus obstructing a path down to the cove which the local fishermen had used 'from time immemorial in the pursuit of their calling', and a path along the cliff to Pixies' Cove. He also evicted a fisherman from a cottage he had occupied for forty-five years, originally the home of John Carter, 'King of Prussia', of immortal smuggling fame.[9]

As with Stonehenge, the Commons Preservation Society, in the person of its secretary Lawrence Chubb, one of Nature's conciliators, moved to bring about an amicable settlement, but was overtaken by events in the shape of the fishermen knocking down the wall, and, just to show there was ill-feeling, trampling on Mr Behrens' hyacinths.

To quote Lord Eversley, founder and Chairman of the Society, 'This was followed by the issue of writs against a number of the inhabitants claiming an injunction, restraining them from using three ways. A local committee was got together and an appeal issued, but the response from the public was most disappointing, and the fishermen were greatly hampered by lack of funds in preparing their case'.

An additional problem was to find, not just the oldest inhabitants, but those sufficiently mentally and physically alert to travel up to London, probably further than they had ever travelled in their lives, in order to undergo hostile cross-examination.

The case was heard before Mr Justice Buckley, who initially seemed sympathetic.[10] At one point he asked of Mr Behrens whether he wanted to interfere with any person behaving properly from using the paths, which Mr Behrens denied. The judge then added 'If the plaintiff here was going to say that because he had bought these beautiful cliffs no one could wander about these paths — assuming them not to be highways — and he could exclude the public, then he should want some authority to be cited for it.'[11]

To the layman, the evidence provided by the fishermen of continuous usage stretching back for sixty years seems remarkably similar to that which proved successful in the Lyme Regis and St Ishmaels cases. However, in the event, Mr Justice Buckley proved to be a disciple of Lord Bowen, and took the view that the defendants had not established the public rights of way which they asserted. He awarded Mr Behrens £2 damages, although refusing his injunction, on the grounds that he had not proved that he had been injured by the trespass. The overall result was that the judge, who had queried the authority for excluding the public from the cliffs, was himself to become that authority.

Again, one can best turn to the newspapers for a balanced view, in particular to the *Western Morning News* editorial for the best account I have found of precisely how the coastguard path was lost.

The learned judge's remarks made it plain that the ordinary law on the subject was far from being adapted to the conditions of the wild Cornish cliff-coast. He dwelt upon the facts that there was no evidence of dedication of the disputed paths and especially that they had never been repaired by the public, as conclusive evidence against the claim of the defendants that they were public highways. This part of the judgement will probably raise a smile on the faces of most persons to whom coast-cliff paths are familiar, for only in very rare instances have such paths received any other making than such as the feet of men have bestowed upon them in the course, in some cases, of centuries of unrestricted use. Possibly, as the learned judge appeared to consider, such use was in origin permissive, but this, though it may be presumed, could scarcely be proved, since the use in most cases dates from a period when no one would have dreamt of asking the permission of the land-owner to give access to any part of the coast not under immediate cultivation or occupation. But centuries of use have consecrated these paths in the eyes of the public, and it would, indeed, be a disastrous policy on the part of land-owners were they to attempt to oust all public rights over them, and to assert to the uttermost their private rights of ownership. . . . the rights of property can only be maintained when they are in accordance with the natural feelings of justice entertained by the people.

. . . It is clear, indeed, that the sympathies of the court were entirely with the defendants, and that strictly legal considerations alone dictated the adverse decision.[12]

For a more emotive, less reasoned, view, one can turn to a columnist in the *Cornishman*, evidently aware from contemporary events in Russia that there exists a point beyond which it is best not to press the majority. It remains valuable as an indication of Mr Behrens' standing in his local community.

These people think 'The land is mine, I have bought it. I own the cliffs, the sands of the seashore, the caves, the woods, the moors, the fields, the streams, and the fish therein.' They, too, forget the lessons of history, they forget that this is the way of Revolutions, and assassinations, of bread riots and conspiracies, of the Labour leaders and labour parliamentarians, and of new laws and new times.

. . . these arrogant, fossilised, crusted old Tories and money-grabbers stand for the bastard conservatism which only conserves stupidity and blindness, under the mistaken notion that they are preserving the pillars of the nation's greatness and the props of their own security. They enjoy their selfish and exclusive 'rights' by the forbearance of the millions of landless, moneyless, and often homeless poor. They believe that whatever the millions may suffer, or lose, or go without, the resources of the Army, Navy, Volunteers, Militia, and Police ought to be at their beck and call to protect them from the daring poor who resent being regarded as pariahs or serfs and who want to walk abroad, see Nature, breathe pure air, stand on the seashore or bathe in the great ocean, which sweeps around and embraces their island home . . .[13]

The only comment I feel able to make is that the attitude complained of was to become much more familiar over the next few years, and has received the most benign consideration from the official mind ever since.

Although praised as 'judicial and luminous', Mr Justice Buckley's decision can be seen with hindsight to have been neither. For the next three months the significance of the verdict was argued out in the correspondence columns of the *Cornishman* until the editor decided that no good purpose could be served by its continuance. It was then replaced by complaints that Mr Behrens was refusing to honour the undertaking to allow free access that he voluntarily gave to the court.

The case produced only one letter to the *Western Morning News*, from which it is well worth quoting.

The judgement shows the futility, no matter how long a period they may have been in the habit of using a particular footpath, of the public attempting to set up a right to continue that usage. . . . It therefore is quite clear that the law is made for the rich, and one could hardly think otherwise than that the public have no rights whatever, and it is only throwing away money in attempting to obtain them.[14]

As to the effect of the two 1905 verdicts on the South West Way, it is almost impossible to give precise figures, but my own view is that over the next twenty years between one fifth and one quarter of the path was denied to the walker.

Not until 1925 was the situation changed for the better, this time over a disputed path to Stockghyll Force in the Lake District, where the trustees of an estate had ordered gates to be erected and padlocked. Ambleside Urban District Council, having lost so many paths in the 1880s, and considering that enough was enough, ordered its workmen to break down the gates. The trustees reacted by seeking an injunction against the council.

The case was heard, providentially perhaps, by Mr Justice MacKinnon, exceptional among the judiciary in that he habitually walked to the law courts in order to keep himself fit for his fell-walking.[15] Although the evidence was that the land had been held under a family settlement since 1842, the judge broke with the recent tradition by ruling from the evidence of usage that dedication of a right of way had been made immediately before then.

The trustees took exception to this break with tradition, and being well-heeled trustees, appealed. This led to what I believe to be the only occasion on which the Court of Appeal have concerned themselves with a footpath dispute.

The three appeal judges were headed by Master of the Rolls Lord Pollock, first cousin to Sir Frederick Pollock who was referred to in the second paragraph. It was Sir Frederick who co-founded the Sunday Tramps club with Sir Leslie Stephen. He was also a particular authority on trespassing, both in theory and in practice. He evolved the formulation resorted to when accused of trespassing, which the Sunday Tramps not infrequently were, which consisted of chanting in unison 'We hereby give you notice that we do not, nor doth any of us, claim any right of way or other easement into or over these lands and we tender you this shilling by way of amends'. Sir Frederick would have made an excellent South West Way walker during this period, but the only West Country connections that I can trace are that he advised the Dartmoor Preservation Association and visited Clovelly.

To return to the Appeal Court; the three judges were unanimous in upholding Mr Justice MacKinnon's verdict, and both Lord Pollock and Lord Justice Atkin took the opportunity to criticise the views on rights of way expressed by the late Mr Justice Farwell.[16]

The situation was further improved a few years later when the Commons Preservation Society's lobbying finally bore fruit in the shape of the Right of Way Act 1932, which became effective in 1934 and laid down that twenty years usage of land in full ownership and forty years usage of land in family settlement would be sufficient to establish a right of way.

However, it is important to stress that neither the Appeal Court decision nor the new legislation did any more than stop the rot; the pre-1905 position could only have been restored by compulsory powers to recreate each individual path. In the circumstances it is hardly a misuse of the language to refer to the present network of rights of way as a network of 'permissive' paths, in the sense that landowners permitted them to remain open when they could have been closed virtually at a stroke.

Such compulsory powers were available in the Local Government Act of 1933, but a circular from the Ministry of Health five years later suggesting their use to provide greater recreational access to the coast fell on deaf ears.[17]

The next date to be mentioned has to be the fateful year of 1939, which also saw the passage of the Access to Mountains Bill, in circumstances that remain controversial even to this day. The Bill laid down a complicated procedure for obtaining access to 'land which in the opinion of the Minister is mountain, moor, heath, down, of cliff', but at the same time tightened up the trespass laws. These last were fiercely resisted by the recently formed Ramblers' Association, but the whole Bill was accepted by Sir Lawrence Chubb of the more venerable Commons Society, and hence passed by Parliament.

No sooner had it become law then the Minister announced that his interpretation of the access clauses was such as would make them in effect unworkable, so that the access movement, having struggled for over fifty years for their Act were rewarded by one that restricted them even further, and were forced to struggle for a further ten years to get it repealed. During those ten years it failed to provide access to a square yard of mountain, moor, heath, cliff, or down. Sir Lawrence's reputation, already shaky following his refusal to condemn the prison sentences resulting from the mass trespass over one of Derbyshire's most jealously guarded grouse moore, sank to its lowest ebb.

It is necessary next to refer to the traumatic summer of 1940, when the coastline saved our skins for the third time in 400 years. Even the official mind was forced to look upon the coast not so much as someone's personal property, but as that vital component of our heritage that enabled the national identity to be preserved, and a changed attitude to the coastline is noticeable throughout the decade.

In October 1941 the Government set up a committee under Lord Chief Justice Scott to consider the problems of rural land- use. Among those giving evidence was Sir Lawrence Chubb, no doubt anxious to restore his battered reputation, and the committee agreed to consider views on countryside recreation. Its report was published the following year and provides the first official advocacy of the South West Way, favouring the reopening of the old coastguard path as a right of way for walkers round the whole coastline.[18]

The committee also favoured the establishment of National Parks, and the Government response was to commission John Dower, a planning consultant highly regarded in the amenity movement, to produce a report on them. His report was published in 1945 and is widely regarded as a classic document. He took the opportunity to walk parts of the Cornish coast, then reopened for the dawn patrol by coastguard or home guard, and advocated their linking up into a 'continuous public right of way of first class scenic and recreational value', as well as recommending that the public should have the right to walk over all uncultivated land.[19]

That summer saw the election of a Labour Government, more committed, in theory at least, to increasing public access, and the new Planning Minister, Lewis Silkin, set up a committee under Sir Arthur Hobhouse, a Somerset farmer and landowner, to consider the Dower report.

Nothing better illustrates how coast-walkers' expectations were deliberately raised, only to be cruelly dashed, than the history of the National Land Fund. This was introduced by Hugh Dalton, Chancellor of the Exchequer and Pennine Way walker, in April 1946. He referred to the original provision in Lloyd George's 1909 Budget which enabled Death Duties to be paid in land instead of cash, but which had been used only twice as 'playing the fool with a great idea'.

Affirming that it was 'the declared policy of the Labour Party that ... the principle of public ownership of land should be progressively applied', he established the National Land Fund with £50 million, derived from the sale of surplus war stores. This was to be used to reimburse the Inland Revenue, while the land so acquired was transferred to a non-profit-making body.

Dalton then went on to say

But I do not intend to stop there. . . . I have been considering future possibilities, including the creation of National Parks and the acquisition for the public of stretches of coast and tracts of open country. Legislation will be required for these further advances. . . . The best that remains should surely become the heritage, not of a few private owners, but of all our people. . . . There is still a wonderful, incomparable beauty in Britain in the sunshine on the hills . . . the wash of the waves against the white unconquerable cliffs which Hitler never scaled. There are beauty and history in all these places. It is surely fitting, in this proud moment of our history, when we are celebrating victory and deliverance from overwhelming evils and horrors, that we should make through this fund a thank-offering for victory, and a war memorial, which, in the judgement of many, is better than any work of art in stone or bronze.[20]

Unhappily, in the five years that Mr Dalton's Government remained in office, no attempt was made to secure the further legislation. Nor was the Fund exhausted within the five years as he had anticipated. In fact payments from it never exceeded the interest. By 1957 it had swollen to sixty million pounds when the Finance Act of that year cut it back to ten million. In 1979 it stood at seventeen million when it was reconstituted as the National Heritage Memorial Fund and placed in the hands of independent trustees.

The supreme irony occurred in 1981 when Land's End came on the market. Although the trustees interpreted the national heritage to include the work of a German artist who never set foot in Britain, no attempt was made to secure Land's End for the nation. As a result, those who chose to begin their coast walk there were for several seasons charged an entrance fee.

I tend to look on 1947 as being the year when the amenity movement in this country reached the peak of its influence. The year saw the passing of the Town and Country Planning Act, which froze all development along the coast and, crucially important, without the need to pay compensation. It also saw the publication of the two Hobhouse Reports, which advocated virtually everything the amenity movement could have hoped for, in particular regarding coastal access. The second Report was even more explicit than John Dower had been, recommending that all uncultivated land, including cliff, beach, and shore, should be automatically designated as access land.[21]

Evidently members of the committee had experience of coastpath walking. 'There is an infinite attraction in the varied beauty and changing moods of coastal scenery ... and a special interest is added by the many geological formations revealed and modified by the action of the sea, and the characteristic plant and animal life that enriches the coast in such profusion.[22]

It was further recommended that coastal footpaths in National Parks and Conservation Areas (which became the Areas of Outstanding Natural Beauty) should be the first objective. An appendix to the second report detailed the mileage of additional footpaths necessary to complete such coastpaths. The figure for the South West Way totalled 96.9 miles, as well as revealing that over one-third of the Cornish coast had been lost to the walker.

It is very difficult to account for the sudden loss of influence of the amenity movement after 1947, although with the deaths of John Dower at the end of that year and Sir Lawrence Chubb early the next year two figures of national stature were lost. What seems inexplicable, over thirty years later, is the ease with which the National Farmers' Union and the Country Landowners' Association were able to assume the role of 'custodians of the countryside', with such devastating results to this Island's irreplaceable wildlife and archaeological heritage.

The change in influence was apparent by March 1949 during the debate on the second reading of the National Parks Bill. Lewis Silkin claimed that the Government had accepted 90 per cent of the Hobhouse reports, but refused, when pressed, to elaborate on how the figure had been arrived at. One part certainly not accepted was that concerning access. Instead of being granted as of right, each individual case was to be negotiated by the local authorities. Only two backbenchers protested, one at the rejection of the principle that a human being should have the right to stand on his native heath so long as he does no damage, and the other to point out that many councils were reactionary, largely composed of the descendants of men who originally enclosed beauty spots for their own convenience.[23]

Mr Silkin's unchanged view was that for the first time in the history of this country the public would have a legal right to wander over other people's land. Unfortunately, after a third of a century there is still only one access agreement to the cliffs, beach, or shore in the South West.

The passing of the National Parks Act led to the setting up of the National Parks Commission, staffed by civil servants, and initially under the chairmanship of a retired civil servant, but chronically underfunded. What was needed was a radical crusading innovative approach to the problems of opening up the countryside, but it seems that radical crusading innovators do not get past the civil service selection procedure. Or perhaps they are so conditioned to stopping people from doing what they want to do that it has taken a generation to adjust to the new idea of encouraging people to do what they want to do.

Long-distance footpaths were regarded as the poor relations of the National Parks, and when the Commission's staff got round to considering them at all, priority was switched to the Pennine Way, presumably in deference to the Pennine Way Association, which had been lobbying since 1938 for its 270 miles of upland monotony.

When it came to drawing up the route of the South West coastal footpath, the Commission proved to have quite bizarre ideas as to its location. When confronted with a landowner who refused to grant access, their reaction was to divert the path inland rather than use the compulsory powers they had been given to deal with such an eventuality. Even if the nearest public route to the coast was a main road with no pavement or verge, that became the official coast path, to the discomfort and danger of the walker. South of Porthallow on the Lizard peninsula a right of way along the cliff-top has even been ignored in favour of a road half a mile inland.

It should be scarcely necessary to add that this degradation of the entire concept took place without any consultation with amenity groups, and the route having been submitted to the Minister and rubber-stamped, all objections could then be met with the time-honoured reply that the Minister's decision was final.

The only bright spot in two decades came in May 1965 when the National Trust launched its Enterprise Neptune, to meet the threat to the coastline. This has been described as the most ambitious conservation project ever undertaken in Britain. It continued the tradition begun in 1896 with the Trust's first successful public appeal, which led to the purchase of Barras Head, looking across to Tintagel. By 1967 sufficient funds had been raised for the Trust to have increased its coastal holdings by 50 per cent.

1968 saw the National Parks Commission revamped into the Countryside Commission, with a wider remit and a larger budget, but still with farming and landowning interests over-represented among the Commissioners. Hence the policy as regards the South West Way remained one of doing nothing to upset farming and landowning interests, with the result that nothing was what they very consistently did. Rather than take on the reactionary landowners they seemed happy to wait for them to die, in the hope that the National Trust would happen to be sufficiently flush with funds to step in and buy the estate.

The most significant year for the South West Way since the formation of the coastguard service was 1973. The official opening of the Cornish path took place at Newquay in May, twenty years after ministerial approval had been obtained. The delay was attributed to protracted negotiations with landowners, but many gaps remained in Areas of Outstanding Natural Beauty which the Hobhouse Committee had advocated completing as a first objective.

In that same month an event of far greater significance occurred; the formation of the South West Way Association, a pressure group composed of dedicated coast walkers with the primary aim of campaigning to get the path back on the coast, where the four Government reports had intended it to be, but an aim which the Countryside Commission seemed to regard initially as 'naive'. My own view is that the Association's most important role has been to force the decision makers publicly to defend their decisions, and because it is no easy task to defend the indefensible eventually to change their policy.

The influence of the Association has increased slowly, but success against such formidable opposition has been even slower to materialise, and a year in which an extra two miles of coast path has been established is regarded as a very successful one. A noteworthy feature has been the support it has received from the local media, who understand that in an area heavily dependent on tourism, any and every new recreational facility is to be warmly welcomed.

The first public clash with officialdom occurred at the official opening ceremony of the South Devon and Dorset section of the South West Way, held at Beer Head in September 1974. It was singularly appropriate that a Tory landowner should have been selected to perform the ceremony. It was equally appropriate that a small but vociferous demonstration by the Friends of Tyneham, who had their own particular grievance over the Lulworth tank range, should have necessitated a police presence before the ceremony could take place.

The role of the more staid South West Way Association was limited to distributing leaflets claiming that fifty of the 165 miles were not walkable, figures that the Countryside Commission were unable to challenge. It is instructive to compare these figures with those quoted in the appendix to the second Hobhouse report, which suggested that just over seventeen miles were then unavailable. This argues strongly that the effect of twenty-five years of access legislation had been to provide even less access than there was before.

Two years later another clash occurred over the route from Kingswear to Brixham, where a substantial stretch of cliffs was owned by a multi-millionaire second-hand car dealer of reclusive habits, and where officialdom favoured a route half a mile inland and largely out of sight of what they had classified as 'Heritage Coast'. Local amenity groups were outraged at the idea that they had no right to look upon their heritage and forced a public inquiry, although it could hardly have been a contest between equals. Evidence of previous usage was provided from old guide books and a map dating from 1906 (significantly, the very start of the twenty 'locust years') was quoted which showed the path as a right of way.

Ministerial deliberations took over three years before a verdict was handed down that the case for the coastal path had not been substantiated. However, this particular story has a happy ending. Following the demise of the landowner the estate was acquired by a body with diametrically opposite views on public access and today one may enjoy some splendid walking along the 'unsubstantiated path'.

In 1977 came the first portent of a change of policy by the Countryside Commission, when the Chairman announced at the opening of Coverack Youth Hostel that the Commission was anxious that the paths should be improved and taken closer to the coast.[24] Excellent sentiments indeed, although not immediately put into practice.

The final opening ceremony took place in May 1978, performed at Westward Ho! by the Minister of State for the Environment. To quote from the *Western Morning News* editorial, which was just as preceptive as that written about the Prussia Cove case, 'The result, after thirty years, is a little disappointing. So, two cheers for Mr Howell and the South West Way.'[25]

1979 saw some scathing criticism of the Commission from the secretary of the South West Way Association at its Annual General Meeting, which eventually seems to have found its target. But the following month, at the Abbotsbury public inquiry, the Commission was noticeably absent, and as a consequence the path was diverted a mile inland, where the coast walker has no wish to be, and, if my impression is correct, the local farming community has no wish for him to be either.

Not until the following year did the Commission actually appear at a public inquiry, over Widmouth Head, to advocate a true coastal path. Later events have reinforced this indication of a new spirit abroad at the Commission, coinciding with a change of status to one more independent of Government. This has led to greater commitment and more financial aid for path improvements.

The local authorities have proved less amenable. At a public inquiry in April 1983 Cornwall County Council unsuccessfully opposed the restoration of the old coast path west of Port Isaac. The following year Devon County Council were more successful in their opposition to a coastal path along the 'Heritage Coast' at Axmouth.

Continued pressure from all amenity groups will be needed if

the South West Way is to regain its full potential, and provide a
recreational resource without equal anywhere in England.

REFERENCES

1. 9 George II c. 35, XVIII
2. *Western Times*, 20th March 1841
3. *A Month in Yorkshire*, 1861, Chapter VIII
4. Letter to *The Times*, 29th November 1902
5. Blount v. Layard, [1891] 2 Ch, 691
6. Attorney-General v. Antrobus, [1905] 2 Ch, 188
7. *The Times* editorial, 20th April 1905
8. Quoted in The *Observer*, 22nd July 1928
9. The *Cornishman*, 22nd July 1905
10. Behrens v. Richards and Others, [1905] 2 Ch 614, 623
11. The *Cornishman*, 10th August 1905
12. The *Western Morning News*, editorial 2nd Aug 1905
13. The *Cornishman*, 10th Aug 1905
14. Letter to the *Western Morning News*, 3rd Aug 1905
15. Moser v. Ambleside Urban District Council (1924), 89 J.P. 59
16. Moser v. Ambleside U.D.C., CA 89 J.P. 118
17. Ministry of Health, Circular 1750, 15th Dec 1938
18. *Report of the Committee on Land Utilisation in Rural Areas* HMSO
    Cmnd 6378 1942 para 176
19. *National Parks in England and Wales* HMSO Cmnd 6628 1945
    para 53
20. *Hansard*, 9th April 1946
21. *Footpaths and Access to the Countryside* HMSO Cmnd 7207 September
    1947 para 157
22. *Report of the National Parks Committee* HMSO Cmnd 7121,
    July 1947 para 259
23. *Hansard*, 31st March 1949
24. The *Western Morning News*, 9th May 1977
25. The *Western Morning News* editorial, 19th May 1978

A FEW WORDS ON THE THRESHOLD

THE officially defined South West Peninsula Coast Path runs for something like 560 miles from Minehead in Somerset around to South Haven Point at the entrance to Poole Harbour. Conditions vary enormously from level promenades to some of the toughest terrain to be encountered on any English official long-distance path, and the walker has to be sufficiently well equipped to cope. In particular, some of the gradients are quite formidable in their steepness and frequency, and there is nothing the guidebook writer can say that will make them any less steep.

As to giving any advice to the potential coast walker, it was Professor G. M. Trevelyan who wrote a long time ago 'There is no orthodoxy in Walking . . . everyone goes his own way and is right.' Perhaps that is the beauty of it. The individual can wear what he feels most comfortable in, go at the pace he chooses, in whatever direction the mood takes him. It would therefore be inconsistent for me to produce a list of 'Thou shalt nots', but after some thought I have decided to give some guidance on what I have found to be the best for me, which the reader can accept or reject as he pleases.

Thus, I always wear boots with moulded rubber soles, I never wear shorts, and when out with my large pack, which means a higher than usual centre of gravity, I take my stout stick with me. I see very few of my own generation with one, and it may even slow me down on the level stretches, but it comes into its own on the steeper parts, and there are many times when I have been profoundly grateful for its support.

As to what to carry in one's pack, the best advice is to be prepared for the unexpected, especially extremes of weather. Even good weather can be a problem. When walking south it can mean having the sun in one's face for the whole day, and salt-spray will aggravate the least irritation, so a hat and sunburn cream is expedient. Wet weather can be very depressing, and when accompanied by gales worse than depressing. An understanding of the wind-chill factor is vital here. If one considers the month of April, which some claim to be the best month to be on the path, the average temperature on the north coast is below 10 degrees Centigrade (50 degrees Fahrenheit). On such a day a Force 7 wind (less than full gale) will cool you down just as effectively as a light breeze when the temperature is just below freezing. Therefore precisely the same protective clothing should be worn as would be considered necessary in the latter case — ideally only the eyes and nose exposed to the elements.

I also like to carry an emergency supply of chocolate and soft drink, although the latter is heavy. While the Tourist Boards would like to see the season extended, it is in fact contracting. On a recent walk in mid-September, on two successive days, I found cafés, where I had been hoping for a mid-afternoon pot of tea, to have already closed for the season.

Regarding accommodation, my own approach is to combine youth hostels with bed and breakfast, which combines economy with comfort, and brings one into contact with people who have to earn their living along the coast, from whom one can learn a lot. I know many people do encumber themselves with a tent and spend a holiday backpacking the path, but that is not my idea of a holiday. The changes of level are too many and too abrupt to carry more than is strictly necessary, and after a whole day on the path a bath and a bed are fitting reward. While one part of me admires the backpacker for his independence another part of me knows that he must be missing out on something.

The other people missing out on something are the record-breakers. Some manage to cover the 560 miles in three weeks, but I wonder if they learn anything on the way. There was a time when I tried to cover three miles every hour, irrespective of terrain, but I grew up, and slowed down, and began to notice things. Perhaps the record to aim at is to take the longest time to cover it.

There are even things to be noticed which no one else has yet noticed, and not just on the remoter stretches. I am thinking in particular of the archaeological aspects — Mesolithic sites and ancient field systems are still being discovered. So when, on the cliffs of the older rocks (Minehead around to Sidmouth), one comes to a field ploughed to the cliff-edge, it is worth glancing down on the off-chance of finding a few flint flakes, which can only have got there by the hand of men. Ancient fields are best revealed when the sun is at a low angle, highlighting the traces of earth banks intersecting at right angles.

Returning to the problem of finding accommodation, my own inclination is to avoid walking the path during the six weeks of the peak season, which means that advance booking ought not to be necessary. This has the advantage of providing flexibility, and one can always phone ahead in the morning to provide peace of mind. The most comprehensive accommodation list is to be found in the Annual Guide published in April by the South West Way Association, and issued free to members. The only time I have been forced to seek accommodation under a hedge (fortunately neither a Cornish hedge nor a Devon bank) was in a location where a youth hostel has since been opened.

My preference for flexible scheduling stems from a belief that there are days of wind and rain when the coast path is no place to be, but in my experience they are rarely encountered on two successive days. If both are predicted (the day's forecast can be obtained by phoning Plymouth, Torquay or Exeter 8091, and is generally very accurate) my own inclination, if public transport is available, is to make for the nearest library holding files of nineteenth century newspapers and devote the day to trying to shed some light on the more obscure aspects of West Country history, although this a pursuit hardly likely to appeal to many.

On the subject of public transport, bus services parallel with the coast are few and far between. All services have been steadily reduced over the years, and the payment of massive subsidies in recent years has slowed but not halted the decline. Even in summer, Sunday buses are virtually non-existent. However, for those of more mature years, who like to walk burdened with as little as possible, there are a few centres of the bus network where, with careful study of the timetable, and taking advantage of the very modestly priced 'Key West' weekly runabout ticket, one can stay and still manage to find six days of coast walking. Such centres are probably only Barnstaple, Penzance, Plymouth, Torbay, and Exeter. Even then they are best avoided during the peak six weeks when road congestion and possibly full buses can disrupt one's schedule.

There has to be one exception to my repudiation of 'Thou shalt nots'. To add even more variety to the walk I have mentioned, but without recommending, stretches where I think the beach at low tide provides a practicable alternative for the heavily-laden walker, although moulded rubber soles are very far from ideal for traversing seaweed-covered rocks. But, 'Thou shalt not' sets out along a cliff-bound beach without knowing in advance what the tide is doing, and without making sure that there is safe access off the beach at the far end — steps do occasionally get eroded away. Tide table booklets can be obtained from fishing tackle shops, and the weekday *Western Morning News* lists the day's high tide times for the principal harbours from Minehead around to Lyme Regis. Most authorities recommend the seeking of advice locally, and yet there have been a couple of occasions when I have been forced to the conclusion that I had sought advice from the village idiot, so perhaps advice that runs counter to one's innate commonsense is best ignored.

By way of illustrating what can go wrong, I will quote a cautionary tale culled from the *Exeter Flying Post* for December 2nd 1874:

A singular adventure has befallen a gentleman near Budleigh Salterton. The gentleman, whose name does not transpire, was persuaded to walk from Sidmouth, where he was staying, to Budleigh Salterton by way of the beach. He succeeded in getting over the rocks and shingle pretty fairly, until he came to Brandy Head. Here, after some trouble, he scaled the rocks, but, contrary to this expectation, found the sea dashing against the cliffs on the other side. There was nothing for it but to retrace his steps. Returning, however, he found that the tide, which had been running in fast, had cut off his retreat. He saw his position at a glance, and looked about for help. But the sea bounded him on all sides except one, the perpendicular cliffs, and escape from a watery grave seemed impossible, for no human voice could be heard above the roaring of the waves, and no boat was in sight. Fortunately, however, Captain Taylor, of the coastguard had seen him, and by the aid of his glass soon comprehended the situation.

He got his men together and proceeded to the cliff, over which they threw a rope, but the wind carried it beyond the reach of the gentleman. A hurdle was then tied to the rope, but this was blown away, and his position became more perilous every moment. At last a boat was rowed within a few yards of the rock, and a rope thrown to him, which he fastened round his body, and he was pulled through the water and into the boat. He had been several hours on the rock, and was nearly exhausted, but on being landed and taken to a cottage he was soon restored.

There are two points which have to be made about this. Firstly, it afterwards transpired that the gentleman was no casual tourist but was actually Mr W. A. E. Ussher of the Geological Society, then in his mid-twenties. The experience did not put him off trying to read the record of the rocks; he went on to write seven geological memoirs and to have the society of south west geologists named in his honour.

Secondly, the last hundred years have seen considerable changes in the numbers and role of the coastguard. There are a lot fewer of them, and instead of keeping a visual watch for people in trouble they now keep VHF Radio watch. Hence, if you should get into difficulties, particularly out of season, you have no right to expect anyone to be around to help you out.

There is one final note to be made; no one has yet written a guide to the path that is completely free from error. I can hardly expect to be the first. All that I can do is to hope that mine are only minor faults and to apologise in advance. The principal source of error derives from the lapse of time between when the author last walked a particular length of the path and when the reader gets hold of the book. A lot can have happened in that time; bus services can have been withdrawn, refreshment facilities may have closed down, and, more important, erosion can have removed part of the path. It is quite possible, particularly early in the year, that the walker may discover that a stretch of path no longer exists, perhaps even before the authorities are aware of it. More rarely, the path does sometimes get re-routed closer to the coast. The most up to date information is to be sought in the Spring and Autumn Newsletters issued to members of the South West Way Association.

It only remains for me to hope that the reader will find the same enjoyment that I have found Along the South West Way.

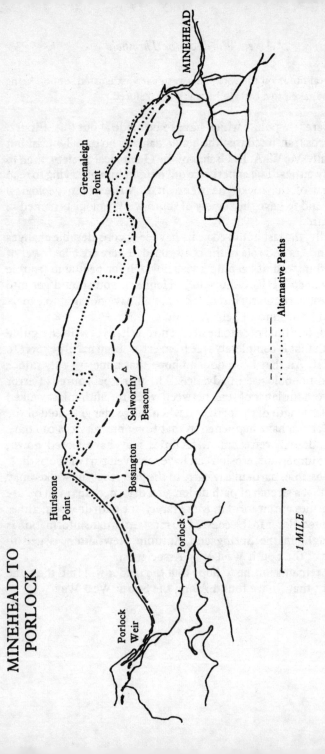

MINEHEAD TO PORLOCK

MINEHEAD

Greenaleigh Point

Hurlstone Point

Selworthy Beacon

Bossington

Porlock Weir

Porlock

1 MILE

Alternative Paths

MINEHEAD TO PORLOCK WEIR

Either 8½ or 9½ miles depending on the route taken

MINEHEAD is a medium-sized holiday resort, currently best reached from London by the National Express Rapide coach service although it arrives rather late in the day. An earlier arrival can be secured by making use of either a less luxurious coach or the limited stop bus service from Bristol. For those who prefer rail travel, the nearest main line station is Taunton, from where Southern National provide a bus service through to Minehead that, at the time of writing, runs more or less hourly.

For the compulsive coast walker, Somerset County Council have provided an unofficial extension, of lower scenic quality, from Steart on the mouth of the Parrett, to Minehead. As Steart is next to impossible to get near by public transport this path can best be picked up at Watchet.

The bus terminus at Minehead is conveniently outside the Tourist Information Centre. Points of possible interest to the walker are that the jeweller's shop window just along the Parade provides the day's weather forecast, but the youth hostel is two miles from the start of the path. A mile to the south-west of the hostel is situated the fifty-acre Knowle estate, owned for the last ten years of his life by Mr Justice Farwell. It should be scarcely necessary to add that there are no rights of way through the estate.

Minehead was the birthplace of John Lloyd Warden Page, who wrote most valuable accounts of walking both Devon coasts and that of North Cornwall during the Golden Age.

Right at the start of the walk there are smuggling associations, which will become increasingly frequent the further one gets along the 560 miles to Poole. To quote Sir Charles Chadwyck-Healey, a distinguished local historian, who lived at Porlock, 'The country gentry had no objection to the flavour of the brandy that had paid no duty, and slept no less comfortably because the sheets of Irish linen had escaped the King's officers.'

In 1670 the Custom House was robbed and things deteriorated to such a degree that in 1682 William Culliforde, Surveyor General of Customs to Charles II, was sent to investigate. His voluminous reports to London painted a picture of laxity and connivance involving all levels of local society. It was alleged that Watchet was effectively a free port, and that Colonel Luttrell of Dunster Castle had misused his office of Justice of the Peace to have an informer flogged.

Daniel Defoe visited the town in 1724 when Minehead was at the peak of its influence, with substantial trade to Ireland and America. With the decline of this and the associated shipbuilding, it found a role as something of an exclusive holiday resort, a label that has hardly applied since 1962 when Butlin's holiday camp was established at the east end of the town.

MINEHEAD TO PORLOCK WEIR
Unofficial Coastal Route. 9½ miles

THIS alternative can be recommended only to more accomplished walkers. With its combination of remoteness, steep ascents, absence of signposts and, in parts, of a visible track, it provides a very good introduction to the delights and challenges of South West Way walking. Those who accomplish it successfully can reassure themselves that they will find very few more exacting stretches over the succeeding 550 miles.

This route begins appropriately down at the quay where the story, as may be found at so many other places on the coast, is one of a handful of full-time fishermen struggling to make a living in the face of large-scale overfishing and rising fuel costs.

A kiosk on the quay provides the last chance for many a mile of a mug of tea, and at a very modest price. The ironwork structure just to the west marks the site of the 700-foot promenade pier, a wartime casualty, that was demolished because it was obstructing the field of fire of a gun site.

The lifeboat station was established in 1901, following the overland launch of the Lynmouth lifeboat from Porlock, but today the boat is only a 21-foot inshore rescue craft. Passing this one comes to the Culver Cliff Walk, with tamarisk in evidence, the most characteristic introduced shrub along the south-west coast. Not so long ago, the grassed area was a rubbish dump, and well illustrates the cosmetic qualities of a foot of topsoil.

At this point there is a further choice of routes. At most states of the tide it is possible to trudge for a mile over the pebbles, and for the botanically-minded there is compensation at the end for the discomfort. Immediately past the rock fall, which provides the first view of folded Devonian sandstones, a group of very rare trees clings to the steep cliff face, with one of them conveniently positioned at the bottom for photographers. The trees are close relatives of the common whitebeam, which does not occur naturally this far west, and are known only by their scientific name of *Sorbus suncuneata*. I believe that here and in the steep valleys of the two Lyn rivers a few miles to the west are the only places in the world where they occur. They are in full flower in mid-June and the scarlet and brown berries are mature in late September and October.

The path is rejoined by climbing over the stile and taking the track up through the fields to Greenaleigh Farm. Less than a hundred yards along the shore beyond the stile is what the maps used to mark as a smugglers' cave, but this is a very small structure, too small to conceal even a miniature of brandy, and it has been quite properly left off the more recent maps.

The unofficial route from Culver Cliff climbs gently under plane trees, passing a spot where some wood vetch grows. This white flower delicately etched with purple is thinly scattered throughout Britain, and in the south-west is virtually confined to the shadier cliffs between here and Hartland Point.

Greenaleigh Farm is soon reached, where the disparate activities of glass blowing, raising rare breeds of sheep and providing bed and breakfast for walkers are combined. Beyond here the path is lined with dog roses and, when the wall of Burgundy Combe looms up in front like a mountain, it brings one to the ruin of Burgundy Chapel. This used to be smothered in vegetation, (including a mass of wood vetch) but on my last visit this had been severely cut back to reveal the medieval stonework. One tradition has it that the chapel was erected in thanksgiving for rescue from shipwreck by a soldier returning from the Burgundian Wars, but this seems unlikely as the earliest documentary reference to the chapel dates back to 1405.

From here one has two choices: either to face up to the extremely steep path up the combe, or to retrace one's steps in search of a more gentle gradient. Actually, there are steeper stretches on the North Cornwall path between Tintagel and Port Isaac, so those who are serious about coast walking have very little choice. Those who do make the ascent will find it difficult to avoid the conclusion that there is scope for a path that is both further seaward and more easily graded, given a more enlightened attitude on the part of the landowner, which in this case is the National Park Authority.

In late summer refreshment can be found from the whortleberries that grow abundantly beside the path. The South West Way walker has to learn to live off the land.

Near the top a four cross way is reached, with the official path coming in from the left, and here one can turn right along a very narrow track. This leads around the head of Bramble Combe, where some low earth banks intersecting at right angles are noticeable. These mark the remains of medieval fields, long since abandoned to gorse and bracken.

A broader track is then reached, which leads to a brief scenic loop before one is forced inland beside a wire fence. This has to be followed for about a hundred yards until one arrives at a wooden gate, the top bar of which slides sideways so that it functions as a stile.

From this point one can look across Crexy or Grixy Combe, which is dog-leg shaped on the map, to the presumably Iron Age circular earthwork of Furzebury Brake. There is said to be a contemporary field system just below it, but I have never noticed anything significant. The earthwork has been placed in the rather vague category of hill spur enclosures, although if it were in Cornwall it would be known quite simply as a 'round'.

Much closer at hand is some more recent archaeology. Immediately to one's left, in the triangle formed by the wire fence, a stone wall, and a small ravine are two more low banks, the one squarish and the other triangular. These are all that remains of a medieval farm. To the landscape historian the South West of England is part of the Highland Zone, which is characterised by the very scattered distribution of settlements compared to the Lowland Zone, where arable farming predominates and where the farms were grouped into nucleated villages. Hence the typical deserted site of the South West is an isolated farm, in contrast to the entire deserted villages of the Midlands.

It has recently been suggested that originally dispersed settlements prevailed in the lowlands as well, and that the grouping was caused by the need to share such scarce resources as ploughs and plough-teams, and took place after the Domesday survey in 1086.

To negotiate the combe, which can be difficult after a wet spell, I have found the best course is to find a path beside the ravine, crossing over it about half-way down. By then a path up the other side of the combe should be visible, starting from the angle of the dog-leg.

The path out of the combe is both steep and narrow, while the contours prevent a closer look at Furzebury Brake. Once the angle of the wall is reached a true coastal path is found, looking across twelve miles of grey channel in clear weather to the coast of South Wales, with cliffs two hundred million years younger than the Hangman Sandstones on which one is standing, which were laid down in Devonian times.

A more-or-less level stretch follows for a mile and a half, with the odd hawthorn and rowan able to tolerate the exposed situation, although the state of the path does vary from undefined to well-churned-up by cattle, until the gaunt pines marking the site of West Myne Farm, abandoned during the last war, are reached.

From here it is a gentle slope up to the crags of Western Brockholes, looking across the intimidating slopes of Henners Combe, where there are only ravens for company. This looks to me to be classic peregrine falcon terrain, but I have yet to see one this side of Hartland Point.

The combe is best negotiated by keeping close to the wall and rounding the head of the valley. Once across the two streamlets height should be gained as quickly as possible to pass above the scree slopes which terminate in the Severn Sea. A tributary stream has then to be crossed after which one arrives at a slight promontory where a scatter of concrete blocks provides some much more recent archaeology. This marks the location of a four-inch gun site during the last war.

East Combe has then to be crossed, the last on this stretch, where one passes through a gateway to pick up a path running westward through the bracken. This brings one to the spur leading out to Hurlstone Point and, for the first time, an extensive view of the route ahead.

The path out to Hurlstone Point is signposted as dangerous, which it could well be in wet and windy weather. Concentration is certainly needed as the path zigzags down the east-facing slope of the spur to pass the substantial coastguard look-out.

In early summer the pink flowers of the thrift, or sea-pink, are much in evidence around here. This is perhaps the most characteristic flower of the south-west coastline, and all except the youngest generation of readers may recall that it once adorned the erstwhile threepenny bit.

About a hundred yards beyond the look-out another zigzag path, not easily seen, leads down through the gorse, the scent of which can be almost overpowering in spring, to the pebbles of Bossington Beach. Once on the beach the geologically minded will observe folds in the Hangman Sandstones.

Collinson's *History of Somerset*, written in 1791, provides a good example of how the imagination was allowed to condition the way in which coastal scenery was perceived in those days: '. . . a grand scene of craggy and romantick rocks . . . the cliffs on the East side of this point hang over the beach with awful sublimity and grandeur.'

Half a mile of slow progress over the pebbles brings one to the point where Horner Water should lose itself in the pebbles, but a prolonged wet spell can result in a spate which forces them aside, and means for the walker a detour along the official path through the village of Bossington.

The official path is rejoined close to the limekilns and World War II pill-boxes. The former are a common sight around the shores and estuaries of Devon and Cornwall, where the soils are notoriously acid, and the addition of lime resulted in increased crop yields. The lime was obtained by burning alternate layers of limestone and culm, a low grade coal, in specially designed kilns.

Both were brought over from South Wales in sloops, which were beached on the high tide. As the water receded timbers were knocked in to keep them upright, allowing twelve hours for unloading before the next high tide. Such a hazardous activity was confined to the six summer months and even then required an exceptional ability to predict a deterioration in the weather. Insurance would have been difficult to obtain, which meant that only the oldest vessels were suitable for the beach trade.

Some more coastal plants can be found along here. Prominent among them are fennel, very tall and with feathery leaves that smell of aniseed when crushed, and sea beet, a close relative of spinach, the leaves of which can be used in salads. Once the field has been entered there are two much rarer flowers that can be sought in early summer by those prepared to go on hands and knees: rough clover and musk storksbill. The latter is best distinguished from the common storksbill by its leaves which are like miniature version of the rowan.

The walk continues along the foot of the pebble bank. Two paths inland to Porlock have been signposted: either can be taken by the walker in search of modestly priced accommodation. The church is just visible, its truncated spire the result of storm damage in 1700. According to the Anglo-Saxon Chronicle, the Danes raided here in AD 886 when the shoreline was much closer to the village. There is a better documented account of a skirmish in 1052 between the exiled Harold Godwineson and the local militia.

The official path continues past marshes, attractive to migrating and over-wintering birds, to reach Porlock Weir. Growing by the roadside are a few plants of tree mallow, another one of the more attractive plants that, presumably because of its sensitivity to frost, is more or less confined to the south-west coast. Under favourable conditions the tree mallow can exceed six feet in height.

Porlock Weir is now given over entirely to the leisure industry, with only pleasure craft in evidence, although during the last century there was boatbuilding here as well as the shipping out of timber and bark, the latter to preserve the fishing nets of West Cornwall. Actually it came near to being a full scale industrial port, when the entrepreneurial Frederick Knight determined to exploit the iron ore deposits on his Exmoor estate. He drew up plans for a mineral railway to run from the heart of the moor to near Whit Stones, 1,400 feet above Porlock Weir, the two levels being connected by a ropeworked incline. Construction actually started (and the earthworks remain just to the south of Exe Head) but Knight's backers eventually decided the ores would not be an economic proposition.

MINEHEAD TO PORLOCK WEIR

Official Route. Faster, safer, but uninspiring. 8½ miles

THE official starting point for the walk is about a hundred yards past the Red Lion Hotel, beside a thatched cottage and some way short of the harbour. Steps lead up under trees, with the path soon zigzagging to gain height above the harbour, and leading to a lane terraced into the rock. This was originally one of several carriage drives on North Hill constructed by the Luttrell family at the end of the last century.

After a few hundred yards one arrives at the Exmoor National Park sign and enters what has proved to be an environmental battleground. The conflict between agriculture and amenity has proved to be particularly intractable here, and there can be few of those who were involved in the struggle to establish national parks who find the present position on Exmoor to be other than a grievous disappointment. The ideas of the founding fathers that national parks would be areas where amenity considerations would take priority over agriculture, and also that access would be increased by the creation of new footpaths, have been largely forgotten.

The source of the problem lies in the expansionist post-war agricultural policies, particularly that of the Common Market which guarantees the farmer an artificially high price for his produce. This encourages him to maximise his output, even though there is no demand from the consumer for any increase, which therefore has to be stockpiled.

The problem is further compounded by the composition of the Park Authorities, which have proved to be dominated by local landowners and farmers with, it seems, just a token presence of a conservationist, if one sufficiently acquiescent can be found.

If this seems a harsh judgement I will quote two figures from the first twenty-five years of the Exmoor Park's existence. In that period not one access agreement was negotiated, while one-fifth of the central moorland was ploughed, with inevitable loss of access. Indeed such was the enthusiasm of the Park Authority for ploughing up moorland that in 1977 they were reported by the Countryside Commission to the Environment Minister under a previously unused section of the National Parks Act.

The Ministerial response was to commission Lord Porchester, a Hampshire farmer and landowner, to produce a report on land-use on Exmoor. As with the Hobhouse committees of thirty years earlier, the amenity groups succeeded in winning Lord Porchester round to their point of view, only to see his recommendations watered down by the Government. Whereas Lord Porchester believed that Moorland Conservation Orders would be necessary as a last resort, the Wildlife and Countryside Act provides only for Management Agreements.

These have to be negotiated with the individual landowner and involve the Park Authority's agreeing to compensate him for the loss of future income resulting from his willingness to preserve his land. In other words further loss of moorland can only be prevented by a combination of the goodwill of the landowner and the commitment of large sums of public money.

At the time of writing the Authority has just announced that it has been forced to reduce its expenditure on footpath maintenance, so that it seems that the best that the conservationist dare hope for is that things will not actually get any worse.

To turn from polemics to a description of the route, this climbs steadily up through Culver Cliff Wood until after passing high above Greenaleigh Farm, at about the 600 foot contour, one is above the tree line and on the open moor. A further hundred feet of ascent brings one to the path up from Burgundy Chapel, and a much steeper hundred feet ascent brings one to the five cross way. From here it is an uneventful, uninspiring two miles, largely out of sight of the sea and too far below the scenic road to have any view of Exmoor.

The South West Way Association have pressed for a more

coastal route, and can quote in support John Dower's view that 'in coastal Parks, a continuous cliff-edge route is an outstanding requirement.' It seems a reasonable guess that whoever did plan the route had never come across the Commonplace Book of Robert Southey, in which the future Poet Laureate wrote of his journey west from Porlock: 'There was a guide for me and a horse. The man was stupid. He conducted me over the hill instead of taking the road nearer the Channel, where there are many noble scenes.'

After half a mile one passes through a metal gate where the moorland gives way to rough pasture, and where there is a view over to the right of the prominent earthwork of Furzebury Brake.

Nearly a mile beyond the metal gate, the track is passed which leads down to the deserted buildings of East Myne Farm. This site may possibly have been occupied continuously from Saxon times until the last war, when the area was evacuated to provide a firing range. Close to the track is a large mound, which according to local tradition is a burial mound, although it is not regarded as such by the map-makers.

Another half a mile brings one below Selworthy Beacon, which at 1014 feet is the highest point in the area and provides a good view of Exmoor, although there is no path up to it through the gorse until one is well past it.

If a shower should be imminent a further diversion can be made down the track leading south-west from the summit which brings one in just over 500 yards to the wind and weather hut built as a memorial to Sir Thomas Dyke Acland. Through the generosity of Sir Thomas's descendants substantial parts of his estates are now in the guardianship of the National Trust.

The official path descends gently at first, with the cairn on Bossington Hill soon visible over to the left. This is marked on older maps as Bossington Beacon. Very little has been written on the history of beacons, and what little has been written is not necessarily accurate, but from the presence of two beacons within a mile of each other it seems reasonable to infer that at some time in the past every coastal parish was required to maintain a beacon.

Confusingly, Selworthy Beacon, if it ever was a beacon, is just within the parish of Minehead Without; while Bossington was originally an outlier of Porlock parish that was detached from the main part by a finger of Luccombe parish which reached down to Bossington Beach. In 1884 Bossington was transferred to Selworthy as part of the tidying-up process that followed the passage of the Divided Parishes Act.

The descent continues with a view soon gained across the fertile Vale of Porlock, said to grow the finest malting barley in the world, to the wooded coastline stretching to Foreland Point. If the path signposted as dangerous is spurned, the official route which descends steeply down the dry Hurtstone Combe will bring one almost down to sea-level close to the path down to Bossington Beach.

The official route takes a usually unnecessary diversion half a mile inland to the village of Bossington, following the path under the plane trees before a footbridge over Horner Water leads one into the National Trust car park.

For those with a very leisurely schedule, Bossington Farm Park is a few hundred south of the car park, while a further half a mile brings one to the hamlet of Allerford, which is the home of the West Somerset Museum.

The official route takes the lane north-west from the car park, passing a cottage which serves teas in season, to Bossington Beach from where the route on to Porlock Weir has been described a few pages back.

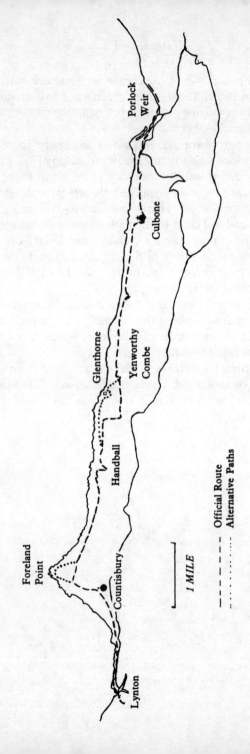

PORLOCK TO
LYNTON

Porlock
Weir

Culbone

Glenthorne

Yenworthy
Combe

Handball

Foreland
Point

Countisbury

Lynton

1 MILE

– – – – Official Route

· · · · · · · Alternative Paths

PORLOCK WEIR TO LYNTON

At its best during May and June.   *11½ miles*

THE signposted path out of Porlock Weir runs behind the Anchor Hotel, but one can just as easily pass in front of it and the adjoining stables and up the steps at the end, from where field paths lead one to Worthy and the toll house of the private road that avoids Porlock Hill. After passing under the archway the path climbs steadily under trees.

This particular stretch is hallowed in literature; Along here in the Autumn of 1797 came two of the greatest walkers this country has produced, Samuel Coleridge Taylor and William Wordsworth, together with the latter's sister Dorothy. They had set out from Alfoxden in the Quantocks on a walk to the Valley of Rocks. Dorothy recorded in her letters' we kept close to the shore about four miles. Our road lay through wood, rising almost perpendicular from the sea, with views of the opposite mountains of Wales: thence we came by twilight to Lynmouth.'

The following June, Coleridge repeated the walk, accompanied this time by the twenty year old William Hazlitt and the stolid countryman John Chester. They were a well-matched trio; one compulsive talker and two compulsive listeners. The journey was recollected by Hazlitt, probably imperfectly, nearly twenty years later in his essay 'My First Encounter with Poets'.

We walked for miles and miles on dark brown heaths overlooking the Channel, with the Welsh hills beyond, and at times descended into little sheltered valleys close by the seaside, with a smuggler's face scowling by us, and then had to ascend conical hills with a path winding up through a coppice to a barren top, like a monk's shaven crown, [This could have been anywhere from Selworthy Beacon to Glenthorne Sugarloaf. At Lynton] which we did not reach till near midnight ... we had some difficulty in making a lodgment. We however knocked the people of the house up at last, and we were repaid for our apprehensions and fatigue by some excellent rashers of fried bacon and eggs.

Points for the modern walker to bear in mind between here and Foreland Point are that the trees are inevitably shallow rooted and winter storms yearly take their toll, perhaps starting landslides in the process, so that the walker early in the year can find the route blocked. In high summer the flies can be pestilential, while during the October rut, when red deer can be dangerous, to come face to face with a stag on a narrow stretch of path could be very unpleasant indeed. But all these hazards notwithstanding, it should be a very pleasant walk. I have seen red deer hinds within twenty yards of the path.

The inconvenience resulting from landslides is presumably the factor that has caused officialdom to reroute the path recently. Just after passing through the tunnel (where my presence disturbed a bat on my last visit) steps lead one up to a vehicle track which has to be followed for half a mile until one descends to Culbone Combe and its diminutive church.

This is claimed to be the smallest complete parish church in England, as is appropriate for what was one of the smallest parishes. In 1933 when the population had fallen to forty-three the parish was merged with that of Oare. The church is dedicated to St Beuno, who is an even more shadowy figure than most Celtic saints.

The Reverend Richard Warner found his way here in 1799, on the last of his published walks. 'The church ... situated in as extraordinary a spot, as man, in his whimsicality, ever fixed on for a place of worship ... those who choose to dwell near it must be content to give up a large proportion of their annual sunshine ... the cheering radiance of the orb of day never descends for nearly four months in the wintry season of the year.' A few people do however manage to survive there today, and there is even a pottery.

In 1797, while staying at a farm a quarter of a mile above Culbone (presumably Ash Farm) Coleridge suffered from dysentery for which he was taking opium. He claimed that it induced 'a profound sleep, at least of the external senses' during which he composed two or three hundred lines of Kubla Khan. 'On awakening he appeared to himself to have a distinct recollection of the whole' and began to write the lines down until 'unfortunately called out by a person on business from Porlock, and detained by him above an hour' after which 'all the rest has passed away like images on the surface of a stream into which a stone has been cast.' However, the fact that this poem was not published or even referred to until 1816, together with the discovery of a manuscript in 1934 containing a slightly different version of events, has led literary critics to be increasingly sceptical of Coleridge's account.

The path continues along a route that was re-opened in 1979 as an alternative coastal path and became the official route five years later. It is clearly marked by blue squares as it runs fairly level through Culbone Woods, now owned by the National Park Authority.

John Lloyd Warden Page described the walk in his *An Exploration of Exmoor*, published in 1890.

... dark woods climb the giant hills, watered occasionally by diminutive streams, which tumble down to the beach over mossy rock half concealed by fern brakes. This is the land of ferns, and as we scramble along the rough cliff path we shall see the spaces between the tree stems covered thick with feathery fronds. What a walk it is! There is no view upwards, and but very little outwards, save where a break occurs in the woodlands, permitting a glimpse of the distant Welsh shore. But downwards, between the trunks, is many a peep of boulder beach, fretted by a line of foam.

The predominant tree along here is the sessile oak, which is the commoner oak of the Highland Zone, in contrast to the pedunculate oak, which is commoner in the Lowland Zone. The easiest way to distinguish them is that in the sessile oak the acorn sits directly on the twig, while that of the pedunculate oak is attached to the twig by a stalk (or peduncle) and therefore provides country children with an imitation pipe.

The sessile oak did, however, have one economic advantage: its bark is particularly rich in tannin, which was once much in demand for tanning leather and preserving fishing nets. The maximum yield of bark was obtained by a system of management known a coppicing. This involved a regular routine of cutting the trees down to the stump and then allowing the poles to regenerate for about twenty years before cutting them back to the stump again.

Once the bark had been stripped off the remaining wood was at one time burnt to provide charcoal for iron smelting, but this was

superseded by coke about 1860. There is a tradition that the
original charcoal burners were lepers, but the only evidence for this
seems to be the so-called lepers' window in the church.

About half a mile beyond the church, and just before the descent
to the Silcombe stream, some very much rarer trees grow on both
sides of the path. These are more whitebeams, this time *Sorbus
vexans*, a species not identified until 1956. I believe it is confined to
this five-mile stretch of coast. This whitebeam flowers slightly
earlier than *Sorbus subcuneata* and the scarlet berries are mature in
October.

The Welsh poppy grows by the Silcombe waterfall. Despite its
name it is believed to be a native of Exmoor. Twitchen Combe is
the next to be reached, nearly a mile further on. A solitary whitebeam
grows here, *Sorbus vexans* again, I think, although I would welcome
a second opinion.

Half a mile further on, just before Broomstreet Combe, a right
fork off the Way leads only down to Embelle Wood Beach. Smacks
were once beached on the boulders here to load pit-props for the
South Wales mines, which must have been an even more hazardous
operation than unloading limestone.

After the next combe, Wheatham or Whiteham Combe, one is in
the Glenthorne Estate, which has been accessible to walkers since
the 1979 package deal. The Glenthorne management agreement is
not a straightforward access agreement, but a very complicated one
that involved six different public bodies in an attempt to reconcile
the needs of agriculture, access, and conservation. The owner,
previously a vice-chairman of the National Park Authority, had
intended to plough up 250 acres of moorland, but under the terms
of the agreement he agreed to plough only 100 acres, and received
compensation for preserving the other 150 acres. In return he
dedicated what is now the official path as a right of way and opened
up the rest of his estate to the public by a network of permissive
paths.

After zigzagging steeply uphill the path passes a signpost informing
one that the Sugarloaf viewpoint is a quarter of a mile off the route
(but not that reaching it involves an ascent of 300 feet). A descent
then follows down to Yenworthy stream and the Pinetum.

Yenworthy stream takes its name from Yenworthy Farm at the

head of the combe, which was reputed to have a tangible relic of the Doones. This was the actual duck gun with which the Widow Fisher is alleged to have fired on the raiders, an incident related by R. D. Blackmore in chapter forty-eight of his celebrated romance *Lorna Doone*. The other alleged 'proof' of their existence is the deserted medieval hamlet of Badgworthy, three miles to the south in the valley of that name, which tradition insists was erected by the Doones.

While some historians have maintained that the Doones were actual historical personages, the idea that a band of robbers could raid villages, slaughtering the menfolk and carrying off the womenfolk, in the relatively ordered world of Restoration Devon, without their activities coming to the attention of Quarter Sessions and thus leaving some documentary trace is beyond all credibility.

The legend of the Doones (which may well have its origin in the raids of the Danes) was one of several that were related around the cottage hearths in the Lynton area. The legends were collected about 1840 on the initiative of the vicar of Lynton when it was realised that they were in danger of dying out. I believe the first printed version appeared in Cooper's *Guide to Lynton*, published in 1853. The Blackmores had farmed for generations in Parracombe and Martinhoe parishes, both of which border Lynton.

Initially *Lorna Doone* was no more successful than Blackmore's two previous novels, only three hundred copies being sold when it first appeared in 1869. The following year the publisher, acting on an impulse, reissued it in a cheaper edition shortly before the engagement was announced of Princess Louise to the Marquess of Lorne, when the book began to sell. It is believed that a large number of the purchasers thought that the book had some relevance to the Royal Wedding. The author admitted to surprise at the book's success, but whatever the reason for it, it has remained in print practically ever since.

The walker reaching the Yenworthy stream has a choice of routes. The more coastal alternative is the permissive path which leads down past the Pinetum, with its exotic conifers topped by a Wellingtonia more than 120 feet high (in its native California it can grow nearly three times as tall). Just before the beach one turns off towards Home Farm, crossing the Coscombe stream below it, and following the signpost to Handball past a bizarre coach house above the Glenthorne mansion. The drive is then followed for some 600 yards 'to pass through a stone gateway surmounted by a lion couchant and flanked by towers presided over by eagles — an unexpected piece of architecture in a spot so secluded as this', as Page wrote in his *The Coasts of Devon*, in 1895. From here the path has been terraced right into the rock, climbing steadily before zigzagging up to rejoin the alternative coast path at Handball.

Those who prefer to remain on the official coast path from the Pinetum, a very wise choice in May or June, will climb up to Steeple Sturt, where there are a couple of seats and a view down to the Tudor-style mansion of Glenthorne.

The story of Glenthorne begins in the 1820s when this spot was 'a wild waste . . . for years the rendezvous of smugglers' and known only as Coscombe, to quote from Cooper's 1853 guide book. This was to change when a young curate on the Isle of Wight, the Reverend Walter Stephenson Halliday, inherited the family fortune. His ambition was to become a squire, and now that he had the wherewithal to achieve it, he searched the country extensively for somewhere to be squire of. Finally he lighted on what was to become Glenthorne, building his mansion on a level plot just above the sea. By the judicious planting of conifers he was able to modify the climate sufficiently to establish his gardens.

From Steeple Sturt one follows the track along to the Coscombe stream which marks the county boundary, whence a brief climb brings one to the Sisters' Fountain, where a lichen-encrusted slate cross marks a spring named in honour of Mr Halliday's nieces. The conifer plantation just below now hides the stone on which tradition has it he was sitting when he decided that this was the place for which he had been searching.

A narrow path leads up to the boar's head gateposts by the lodge, from where one follows down the drive for some 500 yards until, immediately before the left-hand bend, one turns left along a narrow path. In May or June this must be the most colourful stretch of the North Devon coast as the path threads a way through masses of rhododendrons.

After about 500 yards a circular stone structure is reached, said to have been built by smugglers and indeed marked as 'look-out' on the 1842 Tithe Map. A few more hundred yards brings one to a pond, with tadpoles prominent on my last visit, worth a mention now that the common frog is regarded as an endangered species.

The route continues along the open hillside, with the view ahead dominated by Foreland Point, until at Handball the more coastal alternative path comes in.

There are more whitebeams scattered around here which I took to be *Sorbus vexans*, but I understand from the experts that they are a different species, and, moreover, one which has not yet been given even a scientific name. While one is familiar with the idea of trees in tropical rain forest that have still to be classified, it seems strange that this should also be true of an English national park, but it is presumably a result of the exclusion of the public from the area until recently.

Wingate Combe is then reached, and the official path rejoined under the shade cast by mature sessile oaks, although the gale of December 1981 took a severe toll of them. Just past the stream flowing down Dogsworthy Combe two more whitebeams (*Sorbus vexans* again) can be found growing right beside the path. A gate beside the smaller stream running down Desolate Combe leads out onto the open cliffside again, where a backward glance reveals the tree-covered bluff called Sir Robert's Chair. The origins of the name are uncertain. Page speculated that it was named after Sir Robert Chichester of Martinhoe, who 'for his sins, haunts the cliffs of that seaboard parish, accompanied by certain hounds who breathe blue flame and behave, in short, as phantom hounds always do behave. But this is only conjecture.' Later writers have taken Page's conjecture as established fact.

Just beyond, a landslip has forced a diversion above the original path, of which Page wrote that 'to call it Alpine is not far-fetched, and it is without the protection to Alpine paths afforded.' The diversion takes the walker up above one more inaccessible whitebeam before descending past another circular stone shelter, but in a more ruinous condition. In such a remote spot, with the well-named

Desolate Combe behind, it seems most probable that this too was a smuggler's look-out.

In fact documentary evidence of such activity in the area is to be found in the Reverend W. H. Thornton's *Reminiscences and Reflections of an Old West Country Clergyman*, published privately in 1897.

... years later on in my life I sat by the deathbed of a very old smuggler, who told me how he used to have a donkey with a triangle on its back, so rigged up as to show three lanthorns, and how chilled he would become as he lay out winter's night after winter's night, watching on the Foreland, or along Brandy Path, as we called it, for the three triangular lights of the schooner which he knew was coming in to land her cargo where Glenthorne now stands, and where was the smugglers' cave. 'Lord bless you, sir,' and the dying man of nearly ninety chuckled, 'we never used no water, we just put the brandy into a kettle and heated it, and drinked it out of half-pint stoups, us did, and it never did us no harm whatsoever, it was of that quality, it were.'

It may also be significant that there is a ghostly association less than half a mile away, because there exists a school of thought which claims that all coastal ghosts were invented by smugglers in order to persuade the local inhabitants to remain indoors, or, to use an appropriate figure of speech, to ensure that the coast was clear. This claim is certainly in keeping with the West Country tradition that viewed smuggling as a battle of wits rather than of naked force.

To prove any such connection is a formidable problem. The difficulty which bedevils the study of coast-lore is not that those who earned their living along the coast were necessarily illiterate, but rather that they were not in the habit of writing things down, and apart from chance survivals such as that just quoted, by W. H. Thornton, the tradition was very much an oral one. When the first tourists arrived and displayed an interest in such traditions, they tended to encounter the local people in the public house; an ambience more concerned with entertainment than accurate communication; and the stories got stretched, quite often well beyond the limits of credibility. Thus the first version to be written down tended to be a gross distortion, and it is often impossible today to distinguish the kernel of fact from the work of imagination, with the result that whole volumes of local history are now lost beyond recall.

But to resume the walk, the path descends to the wood, crossing the usually dry combe called Pudleep Gurt, the last a very localised dialect word usually meaning a shallow ditch or drain. Swannel Combe and Chubhill Combe follow, before the path emerges from the wood, with the isolated dwelling of Rodney out of sight below. Further down, as Page puts it, there is 'a little dent in the shore called Rodney (or Countisbury) Cove. Here there is a strip of shingle, just enough for a coaster that does not mind a little bumping to lie while discharging a cargo of coal, which straining horses drag up the hills to the farms and hamlets above, and, as the Devon people call it, "in over".' My own guess is that coal was not the only thing discharged, the path from the cove being clearly marked on the Tithe Map as 'Brandy Road'.

A more up-to-date map, the Ordnance Survey 'Pathfinder' dated 1982, still marks down on the beach a shallow V-shaped structure, with its apex towards the sea, and set at the low-tide mark. This was once a fishing weir, consisting of a solid stone base on which was erected a wattle fence, against which the fish were trapped as the tide receded. This method of fishing continued until it was gradually displaced by the net during the seventeenth century.

Meanwhile, the path continues, bordered by whortleberries, to join the drive running up from Rodney at Kipscombe Combe. On a recent visit, heath fires were making the going very unpleasant — not at all the sort of thing one expects in April. Once over the stile one soon comes to the access road to the lighthouse at Foreland Point, down what the Tithe Map labelled the Valley of Stones, and it is indeed a formidable scree slope. At the bridge over the stream down Coddow Combe the official path starts to zigzag up, but the compulsive coast walker will continue down to the lighthouse. Like most others it is open to the public during afternoons of fair weather. As lighthouses go, this one is relatively recent, dating only from 1900.

The Ordnance Survey's 'Pathfinder' map shows the footpath climbing steeply up from the lighthouse as a right of way, and yet it carries a notice to the effect that it is no longer maintained. This is a surprising statement since maintenance of the public highway has been a duty of the local authority since the Local Government Act of 1894, when Lord Eversley, founder of the Commons Preservation Society, was the local government minister in Lord Rosebery's Cabinet.

Presumably officialdom regards it as a dangerous path, which it could well be in adverse weather, but their policy will eventually make it dangerous in any weather. Currently it should be no problem, except that it requires concentration in the walker.

Immediately above the point where the two paths join, some low banks will be noticed, the remains of an earlier field system, but almost impossible to date. Aerial photography has detected other fields to the south and east of the ruin of the Admiralty signal station on the hill above.

Once past the gash of Great Red the gradient eases. The word 'Red' is perhaps related to the dialect word 'redd', meaning debris from a quarry. To introduce a little of what the Victorians called the 'stony science', this used to be taken as the point of transition between the Hangman Grits and the Lynton Slates, but the 1981 Geological Survey Map now locates the junction a mile further westward.

The Lynton Slates are the oldest rocks along the North Devon coast, and are made up of sandstones and mudstones laid down in Lower Devonian times in deeper water than the Hangman Grits. Perhaps one should say here that the rocks are termed Devonian because the pioneering geologists first described rocks of this particular age from the county in 1840. When other examples were found elsewhere it was soon realised that the deformation and lack of fossils here meant that Devon provided a very poor example of Devonian rocks. Only because of the intense conservatism of geologists has the name been retained.

The official *History of the Geological Society* contains an anecdote further illustrating the difficulties posed around here. Apparently in 1866, Robert Etheridge, palaeontologist to the Geological Survey, was dispatched to investigate the geological succession in North Devon. 'When he first arrived on the ground, an active, vigorous, and withal tender hearted man, the contemplation of the great moorland hills, and the folded, fractured and cleaved character of the rocks, gave him such an impression of the immensity of his task that he sat down and wept.'

But to get back to the walk. Continued climbing brings the pinnacles of Countisbury Church into view, while to the right are the massive earthworks of Wind Hill, a presumably Iron Age promontory fort. It is only a short diversion to the church, where the churchyard contains a few sailors' graves among the long grass. Just beyond is the Blue Ball Inn and, if the hour is favourable, the first chance of refreshment since Porlock Weir.

The path continues below the road, past a notice board that indicates the huge rampart defending the only reasonably level approach to the fort. There is a considerable amount of evidence to suggest that it is the Arx Cynuit of the Anglo-Saxon Chronicle, where in AD 878 local forces under Odda defeated Hubba the Dane, thus taking pressure off Alfred, who was beleagured on the Somerset marshlands at a time when the fortunes of Wessex had reached their lowest ebb.

Eventually one is forced out onto the road for a short stretch. It was up this hill on the night of January 12th, 1899, with a hurricane raging, and the seas at Ilfracombe said to be breaking over Capstone Hill, that the three and a half ton lifeboat *Louisa* was dragged overland behind a team of eighteen horses when it was quite impossible for it to be launched from Lynmouth.

The epic struggle took over ten hours, through driving rain, and involved knocking down walls before the *Louisa* was eventually launched from Porlock Weir, and a line got aboard the disabled *Forrest Hall* under Hurlstone Point.

A more common sight along the road at that time would have been the coaches to Minehead. These were drawn by six horses, and were not displaced by the internal combustion engine until 1920. After a few hundred yards one can escape from the road along a path which zigzags down under the trees, to Lynmouth beach.

A recent footbridge carries one high above the turbulent waters of the River Lyn. The scars have largely healed of that tragic night in mid-August 1952, when some ten inches of rain fell in twenty-four hours onto an Exmoor already saturated after an exceptionally wet fortnight. In the ensuing flood whole cottages were washed away with the inhabitants still inside them, never to be seen again.

In all thirty-four lives were lost, and without the courage of particular individuals the toll would have been greater.

An early visitor, in 1812, following Coleridge, Wordsworth and Southey, was the twenty-year-old Percy Bysshe Shelley, accompanied by his sixteen-year-old bride. Although straight from an Eton and Oxford background, he was hardly typical of the genre, having been expelled from the latter because of his atheism. It was a period when he was more concerned with Revolution than with odes to the West Wind or a Skylark, and he occupied his time largely in writing 'Queen Mab', and messages of an insurrectionary nature. These latter he sealed in bottles and cast adrift when wind and tide were favourable, in the hope that those finding them would, as he later expressed it, 'rise, like lions after slumber, in unvanquishable number'. Eventually his activities came to the attention of the contemporary equivalent of the Special Branch, and, the country being at war at the time, this necessitated his abrupt departure for Ilfracombe and thence to Swansea. The cottage where Shelley is alleged to have stayed was destroyed in the 1952 flood.

An even earlier visitor was Richard Warner, on his walk from Bath in 1799, when Lynmouth was dependent on its herring and oyster fisheries, the latter from grounds to the westward. In those days oysters were consumed mainly by the poorer classes, and Warner recorded that they sold for two shillings a hundred. Two years previously the herring shoals had been so abundant that the surplus were used to manure the fields, and it is part of the local folklore that the fish were so insulted that they deserted the coast in subsequent years.

Fortunately for Lynmouth, their place was eventually taken by shoals of visitors to what has sometimes been called the Switzerland of England. Finding accommodation today should be no problem — Lynton and Lynmouth are said to have more hotels and guest houses than anywhere else of their size in the country.

The best way to reach Lynton is simply to take the cliff railway, the highest in the country. It was opened in 1890 under the patronage of the publisher Sir George Newnes, the most eminent resident at the time. It is powered by water, the 500-gallon tank under the top car being filled as the bottom one is emptied so that as soon as the brakes are released gravity does the rest. Presumably, when the oil wells run dry this will be the only public transport left in the County. Sadly, my own progress in recent times has been so slow that I have arrived here after it has closed down for the night, necessitating the laborious toil up the official path which crosses the railway several times.

Lynton has a fairly wide range of shops, as well as the Lyn and Exmoor Museum, well worth a visit in the season. The youth hostel can be reached by climbing the hill past the Crown Hotel for 100 yards and then forking left along a footpath for nearly half a mile. There is a weekday bus service to Barnstaple, and during the summer to Ilfracombe.

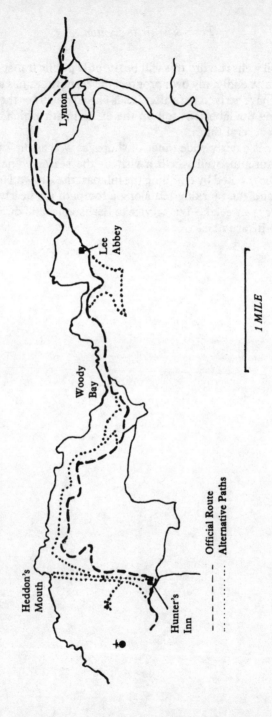

LYNTON TO
HUNTER'S INN

Lynton

Lee Abbey

Woody Bay

Heddon's Mouth

Hunter's Inn

1 MILE

Official Route — — — —
Alternative Paths ·············

LYNTON TO ILFRACOMBE

Perhaps best in late summer when the heather is in flower. 19 miles

LYNTON TO WOODY BAY   3½ miles

THE best route out of Lynton is to take the road passing just below
the upper station of the cliff railway, which brings one to the North
Walk, a broad path cut into the hillside some 400 feet above the sea.
It was actually cut in 1817 by a Mr Sanford, and illustrates the
contribution to the North Devon path made by private individuals
in the last century. It seems to have been vastly greater than that
made by public bodies in the present century. This is a superb
three-quarters of a mile, with a view soon opening up of the
coastline along to Highveer Point.

A temporary obstruction that may be encountered along here on
very hot days is the 'wild' goats which stretch themselves across the
path to take advantage of some welcome shade. According to
Cooper's guide book to Lynton dated 1853, on the subject of the
original wild goats, 'some years since it was found necessary to
destroy them, as they killed so many sheep by butting them over
the adjacent cliff.' So perhaps the present stock are best given a
wide berth.

The North Walk ends at the Valley of Rocks, which illustrates
particularly well how prevailing fashions have influenced the interpretation of both geomorphology and archaeology, since its attractions were first appreciated some 200 years ago. One of the earliest
writers to refer to it was the antiquary, Richard Polwhele, writing
in 1793 in his *Historical Views of Devonshire* that it was 'so awfully
magnificent, that we need not hesitate in pronouncing it to have
been the favourite residence of Druidism.' Robert Southey was
here six years later saying, 'Its origin I could not conjecture' which
is not really surprising, as even today the experts cannot agree.

One of the first to speculate on its origin was the Reverend
George Tugwell, one of several very talented curates attracted to
Ilfracombe during John Mill Chanter's fifty-one year incumbency.
In his *North Devon Scenery Book* written in 1863 he suggested a

61

glacial origin, believing that 'the retiring waters of that cold season denuded her rounded downs and hollowed her narrow valleys, and strewed her face with such waste places of chaotic stones as no mere ordinary decomposition of cliff and scarp could ever accomplish. ... Surely some mighty Northern Ice-King did a long day's sowing and harrowing on this hill-side in the days that are no more!' This was a very perceptive view at a time when the idea of a British glacial episode was not universally accepted.

The first academic to consider the question seems to have been E. A. Newell Arber, trained as a palaeontologist, who in the course of a mere fifteen weeks between 1903 and 1910 explored the coast from Porlock down to Boscastle more thoroughly than anyone else had, publishing his results in *The Coast Scenery of North Devon*, which is said to be one of the few readable works on geomorphology. He was the first to apply the term 'hog's back' to the characteristically shaped cliffs along here.

Arber's explanation of the Valley of Rocks was that it was a sea-dissected valley. Marine erosion at Lynmouth had broken through into the valley of the Lyn, diverting the waters away from the Valley of Rocks, which became in consequence a dry valley. Since then the river has cut down a further 400 feet into its valley floor, thus explaining the difference in levels.

This view was challenged in 1966 when the idea of an ice-marginal drainage channel was proposed. This theory suggests that during the Wolstonian glaciation (the last but one and the most severe — (the same one that deposited the boulder clay around Fremington) — there was a massive ice-sheet pressing up against the cliffs which ponded back the waters of the River Lyn and forced them to find an alternative outlet, carving out the Valley of Rocks in the process. At the time of writing the theory of sea capture is back in favour, although the close proximity of the Wolstonian ice-sheet, perhaps even covering parts of Exmoor, is now a certainty.

The area is now regarded as one providing superb examples of relict periglacial landforms — those that result from such close proximity to an ice-sheet. While the effect of an ice-sheet is to some extent to insulate the ground under it, beyond its margin the rocks are exposed to the freeze-thaw cycles, and the expansion of water as it freezes provides Nature's most effective way of shattering rock.

During those arctic summers such cycles occurred every twenty-four hours, and the smaller of the resulting angular rock fragments, mixed with earth, would when water-logged slump downhill over the permanently frozen sub-soil to give rise to the characteristic deposits known in the South West as 'head'; a quarryman's term borrowed by another pioneer geologist. Much more noticeable are the larger rock fragments, which survive as scree slopes and blockstreams, while the tors were salients of bed-rock that were less well jointed than the surrounding rock, and into which the water could not penetrate, resulting in their preservation while the surrounding material was removed. Here they tend to take on a castellated appearance, and are given picturesque names.

Turning to the archaeology, most maps of the area show hut circles, but it is now realised that another of the effects of repeated freezing and thawing of the soil is to cause stones to form into patterns of circles or polygons, which can easily be mistaken for Man's handiwork, and excavation is required to establish their origin. The only prominent archaeological feature in the valley is a standing stone close to the tea garden. While there are said to be enclosures and field systems close by, they tend to be hidden by the bracken during the tourist season.

Those with time to spare can take the path down to Wringcliff Bay, a good place to look for wood vetch. There is the slightest of traditions that the Romans landed here, an idea that could more easily be believed of Woody Bay. The path zigzags down through about eighty feet of head deposits.

The walk is continued by taking the road westward from the roundabout until below the Devil's Cheesewring, a text-book example of a hill-slope tor, whence a path forking off to the right can be followed. At the end of this path one reaches the boundary of the Lee Abbey estate and for the first time on the walk, those innocently seeking to follow the bounds of their native land are confronted by a wire fence and a notice reading 'Private'. When it is remembered that the Hobhouse Report of 1947 recommended the re-opening of coastal paths in national parks as a first objective, the frustration felt by the coast walker at this point can surely be understood.

Cooper's 1853 guide book reveals that the public have not always been excluded from this stretch: 'Most of those who have visited the romantic village of Lynton, will remember the enchanting spot called Duty Point, whose panoramic view comprehends all that can delight the eye or exalt the imagination.'

Twenty-one years later, when Nicholls' *Guide to Lynton* was published, the situation had changed. To quote from the preface:

It would be a matter of rejoicing to many besides the writer, if F. W. Bailey, Esq., of Lee Abbey would, for at least two days in the week, reopen under given restrictions his charming domain to visitors. It seems a pity that the bygone rudeness of a few vulgar people should any longer debar the well-behaved from the enjoyment of so great a pleasure as an occasional ramble to Duty Point.

A few pages later, when praising 'liberal spirited proprietors', he returned to the theme.

May we also add that no person with the least claim to manners or good breeding will ever obtrude into private gardens and bathing places, or stare into the windows of the dwellings. Such snobbish conduct on the part of a few individuals has already had the effect of closing Lee Abbey grounds.

No doubt it was such behaviour that led the Reverend W. H. Thornton, who was a curate at Lynton in the 1850s, to observe in his reminiscences 'As a rule, however, the tourists have spoiled the country for the residents, spoiled it in every way'; one of the earliest examples of local anti-grockle sentiment that I have come across.

The walk is continued beside the wire fence to arrive at the lodge where one finds a markedly contrasting notice: 'Welcome to the Lee Abbey Estate', but few coast walkers will welcome road walking. As one passes the gatehouse of what is now a Christian Community holiday and conference centre, leaflets are sometimes on sale, one of which has the title 'Lee Abbey Country Trail' and contains the surprising statement that it is their pleasure to share the estate with tourists. Coast walkers denied access to the cliff, can surely be forgiven for thinking that they simultaneously believe in visiting the sins of the fathers upon the children unto the third and fourth generation.

Those who enjoy woodland walking can save themselves half a mile of road walking by taking the path to the left, and following the yellow square waymarks, but the path does contour round the head of two combes and will take twice as lomg as the roadwork.

Those taking the road will pass the access path down to Lee Bay, with the almost inevitable lime-kiln, which supports a few small plants of sea spleenwort. Beyond the cottage with the tea garden, trees soon obscure the seaward view but these soon clear to show fields sloping relatively gently to Crock Point, which might possibly have once been the valley floor of the extended East Lyn River.

Along here a gateway enables a forward view of Woody Bay to be enjoyed, with the Martinhoe Manor House and the remains of the pier prominent, both of which played a role in the cautionary tale of the attempted development of the spot. Just beyond, one passes Crock Pits Wood, where during the eighteenth century clay was mined by some Dutchmen for the manufacture of china. The mining seems to have affected the land springs because after the area had been restored to cultivation some nine acres suddenly slid into the sea.

Nearly half a mile further along the narrow road there is a fork to Slattenslade, which until about 1857 was the only route westward. The estate was then owned by Sir Robert Throckmorton, a Warwickshire baronet, who about that time rebuilt the Martinhoe Manor House and constructed a lower route to it, marked on the larger scale maps as Sir Robert's Path.

An element of confusion is introduced here because less than a mile over the hill lies Croscombe Barton, home of the oppressive Sir Robert Chichester, whose ghost, according to George Tugwell,

is supposed to be compelled (for his sins) to haunt the base of a perpendicular cliff on the sea-shore. He is condemned to weave traces out of sand, which he is to affix to his carriage, and drive the vehicle up the face of the crag, and through a narrow fissure in its summit, which is known by name of Sir Robert's Road.

The natives believe that they hear his voice of rage as he labours at his mighty task; and at other times they fancy that they see him scouring the neighbouring common followed by a pack of eager hounds whose fiery tails gleam like will o' the wisps in the gathering darkness.

There is another version of the legend that is more frequently quoted, and yet for sheer inanity would be hard to beat. It was given in full in Nicholls' *Guide to Lynton*.

Sir Robert Chichester, who once owned the land all around, was a roué and a villain. One of his tricks when short of cash was to attack the houses of his farmers, rob them of the money which they had laid up for quarter day, and them imprison them as defaulters in their rent. A few days before Michaelmas an old soldier, tired and weary, returning from the wars, asked for food and shelter at Croscombe Farm. The hospitable farmer gave him a good supper and a comfortable shake-down in the barn. In the dead of the night the wanderer awoke, men were breaking into his benefactor's house, he fired and shot the leading robber, who turned out to be none other than the dreaded Sir Robert. They tried to bury him in Croscombe Churchyard, but he would not lie still, and took to night-walking, terrifying the whole district. Then good Parson Brinkworthy with bell, book, and candle followed him until he caught him down in Woody Bay, and there set him to work to bind the huge pebbles into faggots, tie them up with ropes of sand, and then roll them to the top of the cliff. The poor wretch has been at it ever since, sometimes he nearly succeeds, gets the boulders up to a considerable height, only to find them scatter and fall back to the shore, then he sets up a fiendish yell that may be heard miles away from the bay.

To allow reality to intrude, the genealogy of the Chichester family is well established. There was only one Sir Robert, and he died in 1627 and is buried in the church at Pilton, now a suburb of Barnstaple, beneath an effigy of himself, his two wives and three children. Furthermore, Croscombe has never been more than a farm and there is no Parson Brinkworthy to be found in the list of Devon incumbents.

Resuming the walk, one follows along Sir Robert's Path for 300 yards to where it bends sharply to the left, and after a further hundred yards, immediately before the Woody Bay Hotel, there is a choice of routes by the little stream.

WOODY BAY TO HUNTER'S INN

Unofficial route, recommended to the surefooted,
given fair weather.   3 miles

THE best course is to take the path, escaping from the road, and leading down to where Hanging Water is crossed by the little Inkerman Bridge, which I believe once carried an inscription commemorating the Crimean battle of that name. The path brings one out on the road leading steeply down to Woody Bay beach (or what little there is of it).

The full story of the attempted development of Woody Bay has never been told. Briefly, about 1886 Sir Robert Throckmorton's heir put the estate on the market, and it was purchased by Benjamin Greene Lake, a London solicitor and Lieutenant-Colonel in Her Majesty's Auxiliary Forces. He was a man of ambitions, one of which was to develop Woody Bay into a resort rivalling Lynmouth.

To this end he formed a syndicate that ploughed a considerable amount of money into the place. The Manor House became the Woody Bay Hotel and included the strangely titled Old Harbour Inn, while the present Woody Bay Hotel was opened as the Glen Hotel. To attract the visitors, a bathing pool was cut out down on the beach, there was a nine-hole golf course right at the top among the Bronze Age barrows, and a carriage drive, now the official path, was constructed to the Hunter's Inn. To provide access for the visitors, a branch-line was planned from the narrow-gauge Barnstaple to Lynton line two miles away, which opened in 1898, although in the event only roads were built. The biggest investment was the pier, a massive iron lattice-work structure forty feet high (to cope with the thirty foot tidal range) and 200 feet long. Colonel Lake seems to have been uncertain as to the name of the place; in the three sets of plans for the pier that he deposited it varies from Wooda through Woody to Wooda.

The first set of plans had been deposited in 1888 but it was not until 1897 that the first paddle steamer called. Many were critical of the development. Ward's *Thorough Guide* suggested that it was 'too confined to have great attractions for prolonged sojourn.' After three summers Nature intervened: the hurricane of December

1899 that led to the overland launch of the *Louisa* severely damaged the pier. The following year, his other speculations having proved equally abortive, Colonel Lake was declared bankrupt.

The final chapter of the story occurred on 15th January, 1901 (the day Queen Victoria died), when Colonel Lake was found guilty of misappropriating trust funds and was sentenced to twelve years imprisonment. *The Times* inveighed against 'a certain class of solicitors' who 'have seen their way to make large profits by neglecting their proper business in order to finance speculative undertakings.' The whole episode does throw up the unanswerable question of how many other resorts in more favourable locations were developed using similar methods.

Curiously enough, there is scarcely a single guide book this century which has thought the career of Colonel Lake to be worth a mention. The typical approach is to be found in the 1911 edition of *Black's Guide to Devonshire*, which spoke of the hopes of the budding resort having been 'blighted by a strange vicissitude of fortune, which this is not the place to record.'

It continued: 'The proprietor now in power has set his face against the developments fostered by his predecessor; and Lynton sojourners may thank him for wishing to preserve this nook in its natural beauty. The pier has gone to ruin; and little more than a group of villas remains as the tombstones of an ambitious design.'

The next proprietor, a Mr Holman, was less sympathetic to the sojourner. As motorists began to find their way down the steep roads, he built a wall and gate across it and decided to exclude pedestrians as well, which antagonised the rural district council and led to his appearance at the Exeter Assizes in June 1939 charged with obstructing a public footpath.

The case illustrates the radical change since 1905 in the way judges viewed footpath disputes. With evidence from witnesses of unobstructed usage stretching back for seventy years, and since Colonel Lake had done everything he could to encourage access (although no documentary proof of dedication was produced), Mr Justice Hawke took the view that the case against Mr Holman could be proved even without the assistance of the 1932 Right of Way Act, and awarded costs against him.

Since the Second World War, motorists have continued to make nuisances of themselves and forced the County Council to hold a public inquiry in September 1961. The situation was not fully resolved when the National Trust purchased 115 acres in October 1965, excluding the Manor House. This was one of the first successes of Enterprise Neptune.

There is very little to see down on the beach, apart from the stub of the pier and the bathing pool, and another lime-kiln colonised by sea spleenwort. Wringapeak, the cliff half a mile to the west, provides the best seabird colony on the North Devon coast, with guillemot and razorbill, but is decidedly difficult to approach.

To continue the walk from the path from Inkerman Bridge, carry on up the road to the hairpin bend, which marks the start of the most dramatic section of path yet, and was, I believe, constructed as a bridle path by Sir Robert Throckmorton.

This section does need concentration and fair weather. If conditions are unsettling it is advisable to continue up past that next hairpin bend to the official path. But the surefooted can follow the track climbing gently up through West Woodybay Wood, or as marked on the Tithe Map of 1841, Slattenslade Wood. At that time it was coppiced and divided into a series of north-east running strips some twenty to thirty yards wide, and was rented individually by twelve local farmers.

Although it is a right of way, this section does not always get the maintenance it merits, and overhanging branches can make it slow going, particularly for back-packers. Eventually one emerges just before the waterfall of the Hollow Brook, which descends from the village of Martinhoe. This is an enchanting spot and more Welsh poppies grow here. The path continues terraced narrowly into the cliff, giving one something of the impression of being a fly on a wall. This stretch is seen at its best when the heather is out and the whortleberries grow as little inconveniently for picking as they ever do. To quote the *Thorough Guide* again, 'To describe the beauty of the cliffs and sea would exhaust our stock of epithets.'

A topographical puzzle along here concerns the 'Cow and Calf' marked on all the Ordance Survey maps, although what they refer to is not apparent, even to rock climbers. My own guess is that they are sea-marks, visible only from the water, perhaps the Great and

Little Burland Rocks marked on the six-inch map between the two paths.

The next puzzle between here and Highveer Point concerns the precise location of Hannington's path. James Hannington's connection with Martinhoe began in 1870 when he came to the vicarage as one of an Oxford University reading party. He was an extremely accomplished cragsman; the term 'rock-climber' had not then been coined; and had soon descended the nearly 500 feet cliffs in search, most reprehensibly, of chough's eggs — the bird became extinct in the County about 1910.

At the base of the cliff Hannington discovered some very attractive caves, and believing that the works of the Creator should be freely available for all to see, he set about engineering a path down the face of the cliff. Initially he roped in a large number of the locals to help with the work, but when some rotten rock was encountered nearly all his helpers remembered that they had appointments elsewhere. Finally only the vicar's son was left, but they achieved their object, and, to quote E. C. Dawson, Hannington's biographer, some distinguished visitors 'expressed the greatest astonishment at the engineering of the path, and the magnificence of the caves.'

Hannington took his BA 'after some difficulty' and returned to the parish, as curate, for eighteen months. He then managed to combine his evangelistic and exploratory enthusiasms by becoming a missionary in Africa, and at the age of thirty-seven was appointed first Bishop of Exeter Equatorial Africa. Inevitably, he interpreted his duties broadly, and less than ten months after his appointment, he was leading an expedition through Masai territory, where he was brutally murdered by natives.

As to the subsequent history of his path, Page wrote in 1895 that it did not look tempting and he would not like to try it, while Arber made no mention of it in his 1911 book. Curiously, the first edition of the six-inch map in 1887 showed two paths with the wording 'Hannington's Path' between them, and they survived on the first edition of the 1:25,000 map into the post-war period.

By the time Highveer Point is reached, another dramatic viewpoint, one is back on the Hangman Grits again. To quote from Page once more, almost without warning opens out the valley of Heddon's Mouth, thought, by more than one, to be the finest of the combes of North Devon. We look down upon the trout stream flashing seaward towards the bar of shingle which the sea has piled across its mouth. An abandoned limekiln perched on the rocky bank overlooks the struggle between stream and sea, and, worn by age and the weather to picturesqueness, is like some old castle guarding the pass inland. . . . But this mountain glen — for such it truly is — is not the only grand feature. Looking westward from High Veer the coastline is magnificent. For several miles what a range of downs sinks into the sea! . . . On the sky-line a pale grey wall rises out of the sea, the Hercules of ancient writers — Lundy Island.

One feature of the scene that was not visible in Page's day is the zigzag path which provides the only practicable route out of the combe.

High Veer Point is also the scene of another equally improbable account of the demise of Sir Robert Chichester to be found in Nicholls's *Guide*.

Here at the witching hour of night may be heard, it is said, the baying of the hounds of Sir Robert Chichester. Away from Caffins and Crosscombe comes the babbling melody, pattering up Slatternslade the cry of the pack almost dies into silence; over the moorlands of Martinshoe they stream away without giving tongue, then with a crash, in full cry, they dash over the steep, and bring the gallant quarry, a beautiful white hind, to bay upon Veer Point. With her 'single' [tail] to the sea she beats off the dogs, till as Sir Robert comes up, and *couteau* in hand rushes to end the strife, she changes instantly to a beautiful woman (one of his victims), seizes him in her arms, and throws him over the High Veer Cliff to perish miserably on the rocky beach.

The walk is continued by following the path down to the valley floor, where there is another choice of routes. For those not in search of refreshment the quickest way out of the cleave is to follow the stream up to the new footbridge which leads one to the start of the zigzag path, although the walker with a leisurely schedule can head down the cleave to cross the stream by the stepping stones at Heddon's Mouth.

Two plants to be seen later in the year are the orange-flowered montbretia, an extremely vigorous man-made hybrid that has colonised the south-west coastline in a remarkably short time, and the introduced Himalayan knotweed, all the way from Assam, which must feel at home in Page's mountain glen.

Those in search of refreshments can, if the hour is favourable, follow up the stream to the Hunter's Inn at Martinhoe Bridge.

There are, of course, smuggling associations here. A tradition survives of a combined operation by Coastguard and Customs men in 1827, following a tip-off. This was a raid on a farm further up the valley. It is said that over £1,000 worth of contraband was recovered, but the farmer escaped through an upstairs window and it seems no prosecution was ever brought. Less lucky seems to have been John Richards, shown as keeping the Hunter's Inn in the 1851 census. His occupation is given as carpenter and innkeeper, so presumably he is the Carpenter Richards whose death in 1875, Hannington recorded in his diary along with the note that he had been in prison for smuggling in his youth. The original Hunter's Inn was a 'picturesque thatched hostelry' until a spark from a chimney caught the thatch in 1895, at a time when it was still popular with Oxford University reading parties.

WOODY BAY TO HUNTER'S INN

Official Route, much less inspiring, but safer. 3¼ miles

THIS route takes the road built by the syndicate, avoiding the path down to Inkerman Bridge, and passing the Woody Bay Hotel before contouring round the ferny combe of Hanging Water. Some 200 yards beyond, a left fork is taken up to a gate and the start of the carriage drive that the syndicate intended to be the highlight of a visit to Woody Bay. Back in the '30s one optimist applied for a licence to run a bus service along it. In early summer the rhododendrons provide a nice show, but not of Glenthorne proportions.

Once past the Hollow Brook and around the point beyond it, a good view opens up ahead. The archaeologically inclined can, after about 200 yards, look for a path up the steep bank which leads to the gorse-covered mounds marking the site of the Roman signal station, excavated in 1961. Less conspicuous than Old Barrow above Glenthorne, from which the garrison is assumed to have transferred, it is believed to have been occupied for longer, although probably not during the winters.

The site is marked on the maps as The Beacon, and some charred ground was uncovered on the edge of the cliff, although it was not possible to date it. When Henry III was fearful of a French invasion he is said to have required the provision of a beacon in every parish on the coasts of Devon and Cornwall. If this was the case in North Devon a substantial number of the actual sites have been lost. At this period beacons probably consisted of merely a pile of brushwood or furze, but in about 1337, at the start of the Hundred Years War, Edward III is said to have ordained something more elaborate — an upright timber supporting a brazier filled with pitch, to provide fire by night and smoke by day, and which seems to have resulted in an effective warning system for the next 300 years.

Resuming the walk, above Highveer Point the direction changes to south. This is a particularly good stretch for butterflies, as the sheltered conditions give rise to a more luxuriant vegetation. Hill Brook Combe is crossed in a wide sweeping curve before the descent through Road Wood to the Hunter's Inn.

HUNTER'S INN TO COMBE MARTIN

At the time of writing erosion at Bosley Gut has caused the temporary closure of part of the path and a diversion has to be made which involves following lanes past Trentishoe Church until the National Trust car park on Trentishoe Down is reached. The original route has been described below in the expectation that it will shortly be re-opened.

TO reach the start of the zigzags, Jose's Lane is followed, very briefly in Parracombe parish, before turning off down the cleave at Trentishoe Bridge, and into that parish, although the official path

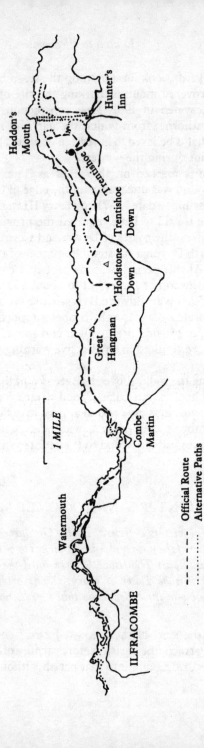

HUNTER'S INN
TO ILFRACOMBE

Heddon's Mouth

Hunter's Inn

Trentishoe

Trentishoe Down

Holdstone Down

Great Hangman

1 MILE

Combe Martin

Watermouth

ILFRACOMBE

— — — Official Route
· · · · · · · Alternative Paths

persists in continuing up the lane towards the church. Some 400 yards along the track one reaches the bottom of the zigzag path, thoughtfully created by the National Trust a few years ago. It involves an ascent of something like 700 feet, but a few seats are provided for those less sound in wind and limb. As one nears the top, the gorse marking the site of the Roman signal station on the opposite summit becomes vaguely discernible. Eventually the official path beside the old stone wall is achieved, climbing more gently. As the summit is approached, a more scenic loop around it can be taken.

Progress westward is then resumed, at around the 800 foot contour, beside the wall of the sheep pasture, with good views forward including the Mare and Colt, two rather attractive pyramidal stacks, and, beyond, of the hills hiding Ilfracombe. At Bosley Gut erosion has forced a diversion into the field. Another half mile brings one to Neck Wood Gut where the rowan trees provide a welcome show of colour in autumn.

Just westward of the gut and difficult to approach is Neck Wood itself where gnarled oaks cling to the steep cliff. Until some hundred years ago, the boatbuilders of Combe Martin used to cut the mis-shapen wood to provide the characteristically shaped 'crocks' for their boats. The tithe award of 1841 shows that an annual charge of one shilling was paid on the wood, at a time when it, and a large part of the parish, was owned by Mrs Amelia Griffiths. Her husband had been vicar of St Issey, near Padstow, and after he fell to his death from the Cornish cliffs she retired to Torquay where she became one of the leading experts on seaweeds. She is commemorated today by the genus *Griffitsia*.

I am not best qualified to describe the next stretch, because whenever walking westwards, I invariably forget that one has to track inland here, and I end up following sheep tracks that peter out leaving me with the choice of retreating or trying to force a way up through knee-high heather. However, it is not necessary to slavishly follow the official path inland as far as the bungalows. Rather one should look out for a narrow path at about the 900 foot contour (or about 100 feet higher than the previous stretch) which crosses the ruined wall that marks the parish boundary between Trentishoe and Combe Martin somewhere near the summit.

Around here are other periglacial landforms, although very much less apparent. On Trentishoe Down and Holdstone Down the first altiplanation terraces and patterned ground to be found in Britain were discovered by a French geomorphologist in 1950. Regrettably, I am not able to explain why extreme cold should effect the digging out of what are virtually staircases, and cause the stones on them to form into a network of neat polygons, although they are not readily seen here under the vegetation cover. They were previously mistaken for hut circles.

Once beyond the bungalows a broad track comes in, perhaps 250 feet below the summit of Holdstone Down, regarded by the Aetherius Society as one of the nineteen holy mountains in the world. They believe that psychic energy can be generated by prayer and stored in suitable boxes to be released when a catastrophe, either natural or man-made, impends.

The Sherrycombe valley has next to be negotiated, and the official path approaches it very circumspectly. It is best to keep to the path, following it inland for a quarter of a mile before losing height. To quote Page again: 'The man with "bellows to mend" had better keep round the head, for, from past experience, I can assure him that a climb of a thousand feet over slippery grass, especially with the sun on your back, is as good a foretaste of the treadmill as anything I know.'

Down by the bridge there used to be a path running beside the stream whence one could get a glimpse of the waterfall, but it has become overgrown in recent years. The slog up Girt Down now follows, and a 'girt' slog it is, leading up to Great Hangman, at 1,043 feet the highest point of the whole 560 miles. A large cairn marks the summit, which personally I do not find a spectacular viewpoint. More dramatic is the view from Blackstone Point, reached by a diversion from the path, which reveals a cliff-line once mined in the search for manganese and iron.

Page has described the view from Great Hangman as the widest in North Devon.

East and South-East Exmoor heaves in long swells. Over the cliffs is seen the summit of the Foreland. Nearer is High Veer, the beautiful sweep of the Trentishoe Cliffs, and the dark mass of Holdstone Down. Southwards the country undulates away to Dartmoor, which on a clear day is distinctly visible. In a westerly direction the coast may be traced to the Torrs, beneath which we catch a glimpse of Ilfracombe — beyond on the horizon, lies Lundy. In the immediate foreground a hill rises from the sea into a conical summit. This is the Little Hangman to which we now descend over a desolate heath.

The heath soon gives way to sheep pasture, left by a kissing gate. Somewhere on these cliffs was a near-vertical path to the rocky Blackstone beach, down which, when times were hard, and even into this century, Combe Martin women would descend to collect laver, an edible kind of seaweed, to feed their families, returning up the path with loads weighing as much as half a hundredweight on their backs. Times have indeed changed; I guess the present generation would be more likely to drive into Barnstaple to buy their laver in Butcher's Row.

The path passes just below the Little Hangman, suggested by Page as a possible cliff castle, and descends steeply to the seasonal tea-hut above Wild Pear Beach.

There is a path here which can be taken by the geologist anxious for a close inspection of the junction of the Hangman Grits with the succeeding Ilfracombe Beds, the latter laid down in a predominantly muddy offshore environment, but with coral-bearing limestones that indicate clearer intervals.

At the next rise a seat has been conveniently placed to give a view of Combe Martin, straggling for two miles down its valley. It has some claim to be the longest village in England. The walker can reach it by following the official path, or better, by keeping closer to the cliff above Lester Point, one can descend over what is now mown grass, but not so long ago was market gardens. Here the National Park is left behind and there is an Information Centre, and a few pubs by the beach, but apart from the church a mile up the valley, there is very little to detain the walker.

Combe Martin has in one sense seen better days, belonging to the category of failed medieval boroughs. In the time of the eponymous Fitzmartins, according to Cooper, it was 'made a borough with the privileges of waifs, estrays, wrecks, felons goods, assizes of bread and ale, and pillory, with a market on Thursday, and a fair on Whitsun Monday.'

The mention of wrecks provides a reminder that one is approaching a 'wrecking' coastline. As Richard Ayton, who accompanied William Daniell on the first part of his *Voyage Round Great Britain*, observed here in 1814, 'They talk of a good wreck season as they do of a good mackerel season, and thank Providence for both.'

What prosperity Combe Martin did see was due to the silver and lead mines, which according to the seventeenth century historian Risdon were first exploited in 1293 by 337 miners from Derbyshire. The last successful period was in the days of Queen Elizabeth I, but several attempts to reopen the mines were made during the last century. Cooper's 1853 guidebook describes one of them.

... another attempt was made in 1833 to work them by a joint stock company, upon a capital of £30,000. Nearly half this sum of money was expended in putting up machinery, sinking shafts, etc., when falling upon a rich vein, and by dint of working day and night, a large profit was realised, and three dividends made to shareholders. The shares by this means were run up by speculators to a high premium, but to use the miner's expression, they worked 'the eye out', instead of proceeding fairly. In 1845, smelting works were also opened to smelt the ore raised here and other ore imported from Cornwall, but both the mining company (whose expenses were £500 a month) and the smelting company soon came to a standstill, and finally closed these works in 1848. Since then the engines have been taken down and nothing done in the mines, with the exception of an attempt, in 1850, by some unprincipled parties to get up a Company, for the avowed purpose of working them, but really to take in the unwary.

With the last failure Combe Martin became once more an impoverished community, although some employment was to be had at the eighteen lime-kilns in the neighbourhood. Charles Kingsley referred to it during this period as a 'mile-long man-stye', while his sister Charlotte wrote that it 'looks best at a distance.'

At least three attempts were made during the last century to restore Combe Martin's prosperity by creating a harbour of refuge, but they all failed through lack of capital.

The first scheme, proposed in 1827, suggested the construction of a breakwater half a mile long at a cost of £20,000. During the railway mania of 1845 this project was promoted again, this time as a commercial harbour linked by rail to Barnstaple and South Molton.

The third scheme was even more ambitious. This was proposed in 1866 and advocated the building of piers to enclose two square miles of water. The harbour was to be connected by a railway branching off the Taunton to Barnstaple line near Filleigh, and spiralling down from the Exmoor foothills. Presumably the traffic envisaged was the iron and copper ores from the mines on the southern slopes of the moor, which occasionally reached Combe Martin by trains of packhorses. In the end these proved to be the only trains that Combe Martin ever saw, and coal from South Wales continued to be unloaded from ketches on the beach, right up until the last war.

COMBE MARTIN TO ILFRACOMBE   *5 miles*

CURRENTLY this section of the South West Way does not have a lot to recommend it, because there is more walking along a main road without a pavement than is justifiable, and it is worth considering the possibility of taking a bus as far as Watermouth. Not so long ago I did try to make my way along the shore to Sandy Bay, within an hour of low tide, but was forced to turn back within a hundred yards of my objective, more than ever convinced that the best footwear for walkers along the tops of cliffs is just about the worst for negotiating slippery, seaweed covered rocks at their base. The seaweed also prevents the fossils in the limestones from being easily seen.

Although some improvement is in prospect, for the time being the official path turns into the narrow Newberry Road, once the main road. The stone by the stream marks the boundary with Berrynarbor parish, and an abundance of traveller's joy indicates the presence of limestone. Berry Lane leads up to join the main road, which then has to be followed for half a mile, passing the track to the gravelly beach of Sandy Bay.

At the bottom of the track, although not easily seen, is yet another whitebeam, this time *Sorbus anglica*, which has much larger leaves and is more typical of the group in that it is confined to the limestone. Several more trees cling inaccessibly to the cliffs between here and Broad Strand.

The road continues to climb, below a hill crowned with what is probably an Iron Age earthwork, up to the Sandy Cove Hotel. It is interesting to pause here briefly, because all three routes have at different times been the main road to Ilfracombe. Originally the only route was to the left through the village of Berrynarbor. Then in the 1860s the coast road was built, and this became the main route until a landslip in 1919 closed it to wheeled traffic, necessitating the construction of the present main road.

The old coast road remains available for pedestrians. It passes limestone quarries overhung with trees, and offers another chance of finding wood vetch. Those with time to spare can take the steps down to Broad Strand, which is less frequented and has more dramatic scenery, notably the tree-covered islands, than Sandy Bay. Continuing the walk, a stile leads into a field, full of tents in the summer, and a descent to Watermouth. Here in season one can pay for the privilege of walking along the cliff and looking at caves (it is a pity that Hannington's views should be so much the exception in this commercial age). This is part of the estate of Watermouth Castle, which dates from 1825, and is now claimed to provide 'Fun and entertainment for all the family'. There is actually a public footpath out to the viewpoint at the eastern end of the drowned river mouth. I believe the circular structure at the end was once a dovecot.

At low tide one follows along the shore for less than a hundred yards until concrete steps lead up into the trees. At high tide one must resort to the main road.

A few hundred yards along the road bring one to a signpost, although there is nothing to tell the east-bound walker that the choice of routes offered depends on the state of the tide rather than on his personal preference. The path then runs under plane trees, providing the May walker with the enlivening sight of bluebells, together with the less inspiring wild garlic and dog's mercury.

Beyond the trees the path enters a field dropping steeply to a stream, where one encounters assorted minatory notice boards. These provide a reminder of the traditional hostility to walkers hereabouts. The next stretch was reopened at Easter 1983 after being denied to the walker for over a hundred years.

In a footpath dispute in 1781 Lord Mansfield gave his opinion that 'if the usual tract is impassible, it is for the general good that people should be entitled to pass into another line', which has been taken to establish a right to deviate onto adjoining land when the right of way is blocked. The one exception is in the case of erosion of a cliff or river bank, when the right of way is held to have been destroyed by an act of Nature. Curiously enough, the Dorset coast has some of the most rapidly eroding cliffs in the whole country and yet seems to have been free of access disputes. I believe this present section provides one of the rare instances of such a loss.

As long ago as 1857 there were complaints in the local paper about the dangerous condition of the cliff path, and a diversion through the field was suggested. This seems to have been the location of which a writer to *The Times*, during the 1871 access debate, complained 'on attempting to get over this fence I was assailed by a brutish man, who ordered me off as if I had been a vagabond. My indignation was extreme at finding I was so hindered in what I believe to be a common right.'

But those who now come this way will surely be grateful for the struggle fought to give them access. In May, it is especially beautiful, as one climbs the slope lined with primroses and bluebells, up to Widmouth Head. From just below the coastguard look-out there is a dramatic view across Samson's Bay to Rillage Point, with fulmars nesting on the almost sheer cliffs. Once over the next stile, one follows beside a stone wall supporting a luxuriant growth of common scurvy grass.

The origin of this name is to be found in the *Flowers of the Field* by the Reverend C. A. Johns (Charles Kingsley's schoolmaster at Helston), which remained in print for very nearly a hundred years. 'The plants of this genus derive their English name from the relief which they afford to persons suffering from scurvy, a disease to which sailors are particularly liable, in consequence of their being debarred from the use of fresh vegetables. Many other plants of the same tribe possess antiscorbutic properties to an equal degree; but these are particularly available from always growing near the sea.'

Beyond, an unofficial rubbish tip provides a reminder that one is approaching civilisation, after which the path traverses the scrub sloping down to Rillage Point where more limestone has been quarried. As one climbs back up towards the relatively recent coastguard houses there is encountered for the first time an example of what I believe used to be known officially as a rocket post, although I have always called them monkey posts. They were used to simulate the mast of a ship during exercises with the breeches buoy apparatus, the more typical examples of which have wooden rather than metal projections.

Once the rocket line had been secured aboard the stricken vessel, a tailed block (or, to the landsman, a pulley with a securing rope) attached to an endless whip (a continuous loop of manilla rope about one and a half inches thick) could be drawn out to the vessel and fixed to the mast. Next was despatched a three-inch hawser, that passed through a travelling block from which the breeches buoy was suspended, the hawser having to be secured perhaps three feet above the tailed block and the buoy to the endless whip. Repeated hauling on the whip back and forth enabled the crew to be rescued one at a time.

The chief officer of the coastguard had powers to order all persons present to assist in any way he might require, but more effective was the formation in 1864 at Tynemouth of the first Volunteer Life-Saving Brigade, to provide trained manpower. Earlier this century there were over 400 such companies, but today I believe they survive only in the North-East.

From here the route follows the pavement which descends to Hele Beach, marking the outskirts of Ilfracombe. From the beach the path climbs steadily up the slopes of Hillsborough. Just before it drops to Broadstrand Beach there is another track that zigzags to the 400 foot summit capped by what is probably an Iron Age promontory fort, defended by a massive earth-bank.

Philip Henry Gosse was here in 1852. He was a first class marine biologist and an equally first class religious bigot, convinced that the Pope, along with not a few Anglican bishops, were inevitably destined to the everlasting torments of Hell, while Heaven was reserved for himself and his minute band of co-religionists.

Yet his description of the view will endure.

... one knows not where to commence the admiring survey — seaward, landward, up the coast: — all is magnificent, or beautiful or both. Let us turn westward first, overlooking the harbour and the town of Ilfracombe, the craft in the one, and the streets and terraces of the other, looking almost as in a map. Here is Lantern Hill just beneath us crowned with the old chapel of St Nicholas, the supposed patron of mariners in times of papal ignorance, then Compass Hill, and the conical Capstone with its conspicuous walks and its signal staff; then come the green slopes of Runnacleaves, and the seven peaks of the Torrs, and the rounded outline of Langley Cleaves, loftier than this on which we stand. The rugged rocks, and the coves of the coastline are seen here and there, and far away on the dim horizon lies Lundy, blue and hazy, like a sentinel keeping his guard at the entrance of the channel.

The descending path passes the miniature golf course, but by keeping close to the cliffs one can, except at high tides, take the steps down to Rapparee Cove. Rapparee appears in the more comprehensive dictionaries, as meaning a seventeenth century Irish irregular soldier. The cove is unnamed on the Ordnance Survey maps, but known to treasure hunters on account of the wreck of the *London* here in 1796. Very contrasting versions of this event survive. A contemporary account is to be found in the *Exeter Flying Post* for October 13th in that year.

On Sunday evening a very melancholy accident happened at Ilfracombe. A ship called the *London*, of London, from St. Kitt's, having on board a considerable number of blacks (French prisoners) was driven on the rocks, near the entrance of the pier, during a violent gale of wind, by which about fifty of the prisoners were drowned; those who got on shore exhibited a most wretched spectacle, and the scene altogether was too shocking for description. It is reported that the accident was owing to the unskillfulness of the pilot, as the wind was blowing directly fair for the harbour; and if so, it is an additional instance to the many which have already occurred of the propriety, and absolute necessity of that class of people being registered at every sea-port in the kingdom, when they should produce proper testimonies of their ability, and give sufficient security for the fidelity of their conduct, before they were permitted to exercise their occupation.

A different version appeared in the Ilfracombe Parish Magazine for October 1904, which quoted a letter said to have been written to the *Illustrated London News* in 1856 (although I have failed to find it there).

It is well known to many old men now living that about sixty years ago a vessel manned by blacks ran ashore, and that the then best families in the town, being nothing but wreckers and smugglers, murdered the crew and buried the bodies on the beach, and then plundered the vessel of a very valuable cargo, consisting of ivory, doubloons, jewels, etc. This having caused some disturbance, put an end to the system; otherwise, in bad weather, a common custom was to affix lanterns to horses' tails and lead them about the cliffs to decoy vessels. Many near descendants of the actual wreckers of the before-named vessels still reside here, and rank among the most respectable of the inhabitants. The people here still retain the name of 'Coombe Sharks', which appellation was bestowed on them by the surrounding neighbourhood about a century ago.

According to the Parish Magazine, this calumny of Ilfracombe society was bitterly attacked by a correspondent in the local paper, who quoted the evidence of a surviving witness that the local people had done everything they could to save both lives and cargo, and which has the ring of truth about it. One part of his evidence explains the attraction to today's treasure hunter. 'As well as can now be ascertained, the valuables on board were contained in five boxes — there was specie, in doubloons, dollars, etc. — one of which was lost in transit from the ship, and was no doubt broken up at the bottom of the sea, as dollars and doubloons continued to be found in the sand years after the ship had been lost.'

Another curious tradition survives here of an adolescent difference of opinion between the future Kaiser Wilhelm, holidaying at the Ilfracombe Hotel in the summer of 1878, and a local lad, in which the former is said to have received a bloody nose. Such a quiet beach seems at first an improbable site for the first skirmish of World War I, yet local people insist that it was so. When it is remembered that the Kaiser was handicapped by an arm withered at birth, to say nothing of his arrogant disposition, perhaps it is not so improbable after all.

A few more hundred yards brings one to Larkstone Beach, once the scene of a busy shipbuilding yard. At low tide it is possible to walk over the seaweed along to the harbour, or alternatively, along the road below the terraces of Victorian boarding houses.

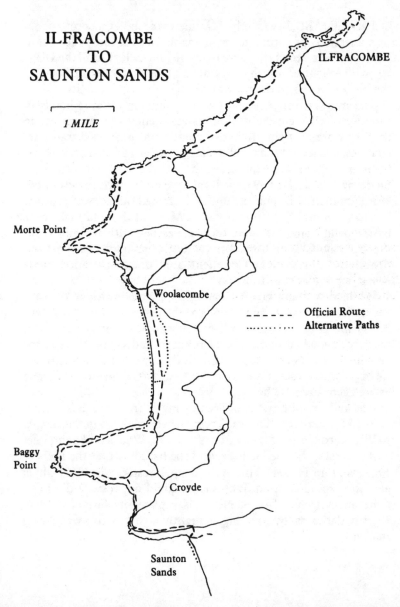

ILFRACOMBE
TO
SAUNTON SANDS

ILFRACOMBE

1 MILE

Morte Point

Woolacombe

------ Official Route
.... Alternative Paths

Baggy
Point

Croyde

Saunton
Sands

ILFRACOMBE TO SAUNTON SANDS
Perhaps best in June   *14 miles*

ILFRACOMBE, like Combe Martin, was a medieval borough, but its possession of a natural harbour enabled it to be more successful. Yet it can have been little more than a fishing village until the 1830s when it began to establish a reputation as the first watering place on the North Devon coast and was resorted to by the quality.

The mid-Victorian period saw the building of large hotels to cater for a still exclusively middle-class clientele. However, as the century wore on rising living standards and improved transport facilities, particularly channel steamers, enabled a social broadening to take place. One consequence of this was the growth of terraces of boarding houses. By 1893, the local newspaper in its review of the year commented favourably on the increased quantity of visitors, but less favourably on their quality. Many of those brought over by the paddle steamers were more concerned with escaping from the Sunday Closing Act than with the scenery. The quality departed abruptly to the Continent, and Ilfracombe found a new role as a popular resort.

While very many people cherish happy memories of holidays here, Ilfracombe now faces serious problems. The trend away from hotels and guest-houses to self-catering and caravan holidays, the absence of good beaches, and the loss of the railway in 1970 and the channel steamers in 1981 have all hit the town hard. Currently its unemployment rate is the highest in southern England, while one estate agent has fifty hotels for sale.

The only public transport remaining is from the bus station close to the harbour. There is a regular service through Barnstaple to Westward Ho!, and less regular services to Woolacombe and Lee.

A diversion can be made around the harbour, past the lifeboat house and up Lantern Hill to the chapel, restored in 1962, which still shows a navigation light. Gosse could not resist a dig here. 'The ancient chapel of St Nicholas expiates its former days of Popish darkness by yielding a nightly light to the wandering mariner.'

86

To resume progress westward, the best route is along Capstone Place, where what is now a gift shop carries a plaque recording that it was here the writer Henry Williamson spent some of the last years of his life. A right turn brings one to the Capstone Parade, cut during the winter of 1842-3 to provide employment for the fishermen, the cost being met by a public subscription. Charles Kingsley wrote of it as 'the finest marine parade in all England, except that splendid Hoe at Plymouth.' The energetic can, of course, climb to the summit, but there is plenty more climbing in store.

The Parade leads to Wildersmouth, the focal point of Victorian Ilfracombe, between the Victoria Pavilion and Pleasure Gardens and the Victorian Gothic Ilfracombe Hotel. The lack of a sandy beach was no drawback to the Victorians, who preferred an active holiday. Even those who confined themselves to walking up and down the promenade were stigmatised as 'idlers'. The beaches were strictly for the children, while the idea of lying in the sun wearing the minimum of clothing belongs very much to the present century.

It was Gosse who described the scene here in 1852, before the developments had taken place. 'The bathing machines are drawn down to the water's edge, and the singularly-attired priestesses of the bath are carrying out little girls in flannel gowns and ducking them in the waves. Ladies are speckling the grey rocks with their gay dresses and parasols as they sit in the sun, and merry children are sailing their tiny boats in the pools, or digging up the pebbles with their toy spades.'

The interest of this paragraph is that it was Gosse more than anyone else who changed the object of a visit to the seaside from one of ritual immersion to an educational pursuit. In 1854 he published *The Aquarium* which described for the first time how marine fauna could be preserved and studied indoors. Two years later George Tugwell produced a book on sea-anemones, and the craze hit Ilfracombe.

As a visitor some ten years later complained 'it is not very much use in coming to Ilfracombe unless you have some little taste for natural history. Socially it is everything here. You are hardly fit to live unless you know everything about anemones. Nearly every house, I suppose, has got its aquarium.' Inevitably, the craze resulted in a serious impoverishment of the local marine fauna.

Continuing the walk, landscaped gardens now occupy the site of the former Ilfracombe Hotel, opened in 1867 and advertised as 'a model of sanitary excellence'. In 1939 it was acquired by the War Office, and after the war by the local council, for use as offices. The result of thirty-five years of public ownership was that it was condemned, but simultaneously 'listed' by the Ministry as a Grade 2 building. Following the inevitable public inquiry, the decision was taken to demolish it before it fell down. The only part of it remaining is the laundry, now the museum and well worth a visit. Sir John Betjeman described it as quite the nicest he had seen.

From here one climbs over lawns to emerge seaward of the Granville Hotel, dating from 1871, thence passing above the tunnels, which were cut by Welsh miners in 1835-6 to give access to privately-owned beaches. The Tunnel Baths House, in the Greek revival style with a Doric entrance, also dates from 1836, but is visible only from the lower roads. Erosion in recent years has led to the path being routed inland of the Beacon Castle Hotel and along Torrs Park Avenue. Yellow waymarks then guide one past the model village to the justly-famed Torrs walks. These were purchased by the Council in 1959, when the admission charge was abolished.

This charge was for very many years the subject of complaints. The earliest I know of is that from George Eliot, who, attracted by the marine fauna, stayed here for seven weeks in 1856 with the friend with whom she lived, the philosopher G. H. Lewes. To quote from her journal: 'We ascended the Tors only twice; for a tax of 3d per head was demanded on this luxury, and we could not afford a sixpenny walk very frequently. Yet the view is perhaps the finest to be had at Ilfracombe. Bay behind bay, fringed with foam, and promontory behind promontory, each with its peculiar shades of purple light — the sweep of the Wesh coast faintly visible in the distance, and the endless expanse of sea . . .'

In their pursuit of marine fauna they were assisted by the Reverend Tugwell. One of her letters referred to 'the little zoological curate, who is really one of the best specimens of the clergyman species I have seen.' I wonder if he would have been so cordial had he known their real status.

Continuing westwards, just before the zigzags there is a narrow green promontory called Torrs Point. Gosse was here and provides us with a glimpse of the Victorians' obsession before he converted them to the quest for zoophytes.

From near the middle of the western side, a zigzag staircase of steps, rudely cut in the living rock, leads down the face of the lofty cliff . . . By clambering over piled masses . . . I found myself in White Pebble Bay. . . . This little bay is one of the few recognised localities for the true maidenhair fern; and it so happened that while I was looking about to discover a specimen on the cliffs, I met with a gentleman who was here with the same object. He, however, was better instructed where to procure it, and how; for he had brought servants with him, and had taken the trouble to provide himself with a ladder, which he had reared against the side of a glen . . . Here, some fifteen or twenty feet up, . . . grows the maidenhair in little tufts, to obtain which without injury, it is necessary to detach fragments of the rock with a hammer.

Perhaps by diverting the Victorians' abundant energy Gosse managed to save some of our rarer ferns. George Tugwell wrote in 1863 that 'the maidenhair fern had been almost eradicated by dealers and tourists, and the sea fern will probably soon share the same fate.' This illustrates the complete change in attitudes since those days. I believe the maidenhair fern survives in inaccessible spots around here although on the south coast it grows near the path down to a popular beach, while the sea spleenwort referred to above as sea fern is hardly considered attractive today.

Having ascended the zigzags, one arrives at the summit of the seven hills, although there seems to be room for argument as to which the other six are. There used to be a pavilion and restaurant here, of which Page wrote disparagingly that it was 'a large glass refreshment house surrounded by a bristling array of automatic machines . . . evidence of the inevitable cockneyfying which everywhere, nowadays, overtakes the fashionable watering place'. He went on to express the wish that 'a new generation shall arise that knows not the cockney, that insists on relegating such monstrosities to a humbler position.' His wish was to some extent fulfilled some sixty-five years later when the offending structure was demolished.

Nearly all the coastline from here along to Croyde Bay is in the safe keeping of the National Trust, but, most unusually, there is very little true cliff path for the next two miles, and one has to trend inland to pick up the old road to Lee.

The 1981 Geological Map shows that one is now on the Morte Slates, younger and more glossy than the Ilfracombe Slates. Several books claim that the two formations give rise to contrasting scenery. The Morte Slates are said to provide a more rounded inland topography, in contrast to the craggier Ilfracombe Beds, although they give rise to a coastline consisting of nearly vertical sharp-edged reefs, known locally as the 'cruel Morte Slates'. The differences between the two formations can hardly be very marked, because some earlier writers have taken the junction of the two formations to be a mile further to the west.

As the gradient eases one passes a cast iron sign reading uncompromisingly 'Public Path Please Keep To It'. It looks Victorian and could well be, as the Barnstaple foundry which produced it functioned from about 1875 to 1908. Sheep pasture slopes down towards Flat Point, and it looks as if it had always been sheep pasture, yet the Tithe Map of 1840 shows all of the next 500 yards to have been arable land cultivated on the strip system.

The route continues more or less level until the lane is reached. Here fuchsia is in evidence to remind the walker that he is approaching Lee, in what used to be called Fuchsia Valley. Just below the third house, Silvercove, it is possible to peer through the privet hedge and discern in the corner of the field a standing stone of white quartz, over four feet high. This is one of what used to be four standing stones in the area. None of the stones is marked on any map.

The purpose of standing stones remains a subject of speculation. In 1861 James Davidson, the East Devon antiquary, listed the possibilities. 'Whether they were Druidical monuments, bound-stones, memorials of battle-fields, sepulchral monuments, way-marks on ancient roads or otherwise, must be left to the local investigator, with history, tradition, and actual inspection for his guides.' The examples here have now been tentatively dated to the later Neolithic period, following work in Wiltshire involving actual excavation of standing stones.

There is said to be another standing stone in the middle of the second field below the first stone, and also said to be visible from a mile away. But even when armed with the eight-figure grid reference from the County Sites and Monuments Register I have been unable to find it, so either it is no longer there or Nature did not intend me to be a field archaeologist. There is also said to be a third lying on top of the hedge bank — hardly a standing stone — by the junction with Home Lane, just on the left, and the broken quartz in the hedge of the field opposite is said to derive from a fourth.

At a suitable hour the bibulous walker can divert himself down Home Lane in the direction of the Grampus, which was opened in 1975 in allegedly fourteenth century buildings.Meanwhile the official path continues steeply down the narrow lane to the rocky beach of Lee, dominated by a large hotel.

To the right of the beach is the Old Mill, now a listed building, and once worked by a leat that ran down the lane beside the hotel. It was the scene of the remarkable wreck of the *William Wilberforce* on October 23rd, 1842, of which contrasting accounts survive. This is Gosse's decription: 'It seemed incredible that under any circumstance of tempest or tide, a vessel of size could be carried to the spot where I was standing. Yet if trustworthy persons are to be trusted, a brig was a few years ago lifted by the violence of the surf clean over the floor of rocks, and lodged high and dry here by the side of the mill. The crew, it is supposed, had in despair taken to their boat previously, and were all unhappily drowned, their precaution proving their destruction.'

This version is supported by the contemporary account given in the *Exeter Flying Post*. To quote very briefly from it, 'during a heavy gale, and whilst a high sea was running, a brig called the *William Wilberforce* drove ashore in Lee Bay ... The vessel was seen by a man coming from Mortehoe apparently steering for the harbour of Ilfracombe; but on his arrival at Lee, to his surprise, he saw her on the rocks. ... An inquest has been held on the six bodies picked up, and a verdict returned of "found drowned".'

A vastly different account is given by the Reverend John Mill Chanter, brother-in-law of Charles Kingsley and vicar of Ilfracombe from 1836 to 1887, in his *Wanderings in North Devon*, written during the latter year.

In the old days the evil practice of 'wrecking' was carried on to a terrible extent all along the coast. One method of enticing vessels ashore, was to place lights in different spots along the cliffs. If the vessel was a foreigner, or without a pilot, it would often make for the light, the crew thinking it was placed there to guide them in. The *William Wilberforce* which was wrecked at Lee, gives a terrible instance of the villainy of which the 'wreckers' were capable. One Sunday night when the people were in Church, and a gale from the north-west was raging wildly round its walls, and at times quite drowning the voice of the preacher, the shrill note of a whistle was heard outside the door; the startled congregation gazed at each other, and the Coastguards hurriedly rose and left the Church. Mr Cockbourn, their captain, was waiting for them outside; there was a brig ashore at Lee, and they must hurry there at once and see what could be done. But nothing could be done, for the crew were all drowned, seven lives altogether. The vessel was a timberman from America and was supposed to have been wilfully lured ashore by a man called Q., who had tied a lantern on to his donkey's tail to make it appear to the helmsman that he was perfectly free from the rocks with plenty of sea-room. The action of the donkey on the beach caused the lantern to move up and down, just as a shiplight would by the action of the waves, so causing the poor creatures to think there were vessels anchored between them and the shore.

This is a very good story, but the facts do not bear it out: according to the *Flying Post* the vessel was bound from Milford Haven for London carrying coal, and a contemporary account has to be preferred to one recollected forty-five years on.

At the other end of the beach is another listed building, Smugglers Cottage, bearing the date 1627. The smuggling tradition here is certainly more substantial than the wrecking tradition. To quote a local journalist of the last century, 'Lee had quite a reputation for smuggling in the "good old days" when to cheat the King and rob the King's revenue was counted but a show of reciprocity.' One name in particular stands out, that of Hannibal Richards, who is said to have been born at Morwenstow and to have served his apprenticeship with the Coppinger gang. He appears in the 1841 census very appropriately as the publican. It seems to have been a very healthy life — both his wife and daughter lived to a hundred.

Their headstone can still be seen beside the path in Ilfracombe churchyard.

The walk is continued steeply up the lane for a few hundred yards before steps lead along the slope of what used to be called Flagstaff Hill until the flagstaff was struck by lightning in 1952. An even older name is Warborough Hill, which is usually derived from the Old English *ward-beorg*, meaning a watch-hill. Yet it seems a curious site for a look-out, being dominated by higher cliffs on both sides, which restricts the view down the channel to the northern half of Lundy.

In contrast, the Warborough on the South Devon coast is the start of a chain of similarly-named hills, each one visible from its neighbour, the line leading to the nearest Saxon fortified borough; but I know of no other example in North Devon.

To resume the walk, a path has recently been created closer to the cliff-edge, passing the near-vertical path down to Sandy Cove, where Hannibal Richards is said to have had a secret cave. In fact the old six-inch map marks Brandy Cave on the little promontory to the west.

After crossing the stream running down to Hilly Mouth and climbing to the summit of Damaghue Cliff, one may divert to the little eminence about fifty yards to the left of the path. Here there are two more standing stones to be seen, one due south in the next field, and another half-hidden among the gorse on the sky-line just to the right. A third one, curiously hook-shaped, is located out of sight some 200 yards south of the latter.

The valley running down to Bennett's Mouth has now to be crossed by means of a new footbridge and the new style of National Trust stile featuring a lifting section to enable dogs to pass under. Having regained the 200 feet contour one soon arrives at Bull Point lighthouse opened in 1879 to protect shipping from the 'cruel Morte Slates'.

The lighthouse faithfully served the maritime community for ninety-three years until one day in September 1972 some hundred feet of cliff suddenly slipped into the sea; fissures appeared within the boundary wall and the fog signal was put out of action. A temporary light had to be hurriedly borrowed while the lighthouse was rebuilt further inland. It was re-opened in 1975 and made fully automatic, the function of the keeper being to monitor the computerised system.

The footpath along here is not well defined by National Trust standards, although it is an Enterprise Neptune success. Perhaps officialdom is fearful of a further landslip. The route continues to undulate, passing above Rockham Beach, sandy at low tide, and with the metal ribs of a wreck visible on my last visit.

From here it is just over a mile to Morte Point, and a dramatic change of direction and scenery. The Point overlooks the Morte Stone, innocent enough on a sunny day, but the Rock of Death was no misnomer during the last century. To quote some particularly flowery prose from a journalist of that period: 'a passing acquaintance with the wreck lore of this deadly seaboard will suffice to conjure up in our imagination the harrowing scenes of which this sea-monster has been the unwitting cause. A fog-bound coast, a pilot miscalculating his drift-way, and no guide to distance from the land — and the merciless Morte Stone would ever and anon see a fresh sacrifice. Until the sea gives up its myriad dead the history of this dread spot will remain in faint conception.'

Once around the promontory a pleasanter prospect opens up; the two mile stretch of Woolacombe Sands, the best beach yet encountered, with the inevitable holiday development at each end. Virtually all the buildings date from the present century. The situation was too exposed to support a fishing community, or even to appeal to the Victorian holiday-maker.

Perhaps it was also too exposed for smuggling, which might explain why there is very much a 'wrecking' tradition along here. As Charles Kingsley put it, writing in 1849, 'Wild Folk are these here, gatherers of shellfish and laver, and merciless to wrecked vessels, which they consider as their own by immemorial usage, or rather right divine. Significant, how an agricultural people is generally as cruel to wrecked seamen, as a fishing one is merciful. I could tell you twenty stories of the baysmen down there to the westward risking themselves like very heroes to save strangers' lives, and beating off the labouring folk who swarmed down for plunder from the inland hills.'

Just before the path climbs steeply up towards the road is Grunta Beach, which tradition says derived its name from the wreck here of a vessel laden with pigs.

Botanically, things improve, with the introduced silver ragwort and, as one passes seaward of the houses, tree mallow. A short stretch of road follows down past the Watersmeet Hotel. Beyond, one is above Combegate Beach, a gate across the road here, at the bottom of Twitchen Combe, surviving into the present century.

Another 400 yards brings one to the concrete look-out above Barricane Beach, which was a considerable attraction to the day trippers from Victorian Ilfracombe. To quote from Gosse again:

Its peculiarity is that it has a beach entirely composed of shells, some of which are rare, or at least are not found anywhere else in this vicinity. . . . from the grassy slopes at the top of the cliffs a narrow path leads steeply down to an area of what seems to be small pebbles; but which, on examination, prove to be shells of many kinds. Most of these, having been washed up by the tides, are broken into fragments; but a good number are found in tolerable integrity. Groups of women and girls from the neighbouring hamlets may always be seen, during the summer months, raking with their fingers among the fragments, for unbroken specimens; collections of which they offer for sale to visitors.

Nowadays the ocean currents no longer bring exotic specimens from the Caribbean as it was said they did in Gosse's day. He also wrote something else about the beach and the subject of wrecking, which he published three years later:

Women, no less than men, are ready to engage in these lawless deeds; and in the horrible tales which are whispered in the neighbourhood, of violence and even murder perpetrated upon poor shipwrecked mariners; women, strange to say, commonly play the most prominent part. It is hoped that matters do not now proceed to such dreadful extremities as these. The present generation well remembers a wretched woman, Bayle by name, who was reputed to have murdered one Captain Harry, the master of a trading vessel, which had run ashore on Woolacombe Sands. The captain had struggled to the rocks at Barricane, where he lay exhausted; when this vile woman, coming up with her 'pick', a sort of pitchfork in her hand, is said to have pushed him back into the sea, and to have kept him under water with the iron prongs, until he was drowned. Tradition states that remorse overcame her reason, and that she died a maniac. It is right

to add, however, that a respectable inhabitant of Morte, who remembers
the woman well, told me that he thought the imputation of the crime
rested on insufficient evidence.

The little volume in which this account occurs is rather unaptly
entitled *Seaside Pleasures*. As a story it belongs to the category of
those that can never be disproved, but my own opinion is that its
origin is to be sought in some relatively trivial incident, grotesquely
distorted and whispered loudly enough for the diversion (in both
senses) of the credulous tourist. If my analysis is correct, one could
expect the story to be even further distorted with the passage of
time, and, sure enough, in the 1920s Henry Williamson was regaled,
in a public bar, with the story of Captain 'Arry riding headless on a
white horse in the south-west gales.

As to the original incident, it need have been nothing more
dramatic than the following, gleaned from the pages of the *North
Devon Journal* for February 21st, 1850.

Caution to Wreckers — notwithstanding the vigilance of the Receiver for
Droits of Admiralty (Mr William Huxtable, Ilfracombe), whose district
extends from Baggy Point to Porlock Point, and whose resolute and
fearless conduct towards those dastardly robbers, or free booters, called
'wreckers', renders his position frequently one of danger, and therefore
calls for every support from the authorities, he has for some time past
found it necessary to threaten parties with the law, not only around
Mortehoe, but at Ilfracombe; and the following flagrant case having
occurred, and the person being a known depredator, he was induced to
make an example of her. — On Friday morning last, a vessel was
discovered on shore on the Barricane rocks by a labourer going from
Mortehoe to Woolacombe Barton. There was a dense fog at the time, and
he could hardly see that it was a vessel, but he informed his employer,
who sent his son to Ilfracombe to apprise Mr Huxtable of the circumstances.
The latter immediately proceeded to the spot, but found the unfortunate
vessel had gone to pieces before his arrival. Her name was the *William and
Jane*, a smack belonging to Barnstaple.

Mr Huxtable gave instructions for saving spars, sails, anchors, chains,
etc., and which were sold on Tuesday last for the benefit of those
concerned. Midway between Mortehoe church and the Barricane Rocks,

Mr Huxtable met a person of the name of Elizabeth Berry, of whom he enquired what she had in the sack she was carrying. She replied, 'Only a bit of timber'. Suspecting, however, that she was telling a falsehood, he desired her to turn it out, which she most reluctantly did, when it proved to be a tub and a bed sack, belonging to one of the crew. Under the circumstances therefore, and from the woman's impertinence and evasive replies, Mr Huxtable felt that he was called upon to have her taken before a magistrate, and accordingly she appeared on Saturday last before Nathaniel Vye, Esq., but the full hearing was adjourned till Monday, when Mr Vye, after a careful investigation of the case, and the master identifying the articles in question, convicted Mrs Berry in the penalty of one pound, which on failing to pay, she was committed for twenty-one days to prison, where it is hoped that a little hard labour, with prison discipline, will warn her and others against such dastardly conduct, in taking away from unfortunate mariners, especially those lying dead on the shore, any part of their property.

The following week the editor returned to the theme.

The dreadful practice of 'Wrecking', so common on the coasts of the most barbarous parts of our own and some other countries, it is sad to find still disgracing this neighbourhood. This most wicked practice (in some of its features even more horrible than the deeds of the highwayman) is nevertheless carried on, apparently without any check of conscience, by persons who would start with horror at acting the part of the footpad. The detection, conviction, and punishment of the individual, reported in this paper last week, it might have been thought would have deterred any other parties, for the present at least, from the repetition of a similar crime: yet on Saturday morning last, about 3 a.m., six men were discovered doing their best to walk off with a bowsprit, a part of the late wreck, and which had been sold at the sale a day or two previously. A man had been set to watch by Mr Huxtable, Lloyd's agent at Ilfracombe, at the cottage near which the wreck had been deposited. His attention was attracted to some out of door proceedings at the time stated, when he and the man of the house turned out to see what was up, and found the bowsprit walking off on those six pairs of thievish legs. Unfortunately the scamps became aware that they were observed, dropped their load, and scampered off, escaping for the present, we regret to add, the gripe of justice, which they so richly deserve to feel.

To resume the walk, one can progress seaward of the road, over well-worn grass, until by some red-brick toilets a path, not easily seen, descends to the beach, which (except at high tide) can be followed all the way to Putsborough. However, personally, I find beach walking monotonous, and prefer part of the official route, which means getting off the beach by the boat-house café, once the home of Morthoe's lifeboat. The impossibility of launching in a westerly gale meant that it had achieved only one successful service in thirty years when the decision to close it was taken in 1900.

When the lifeboat station was opened Woolacombe consisted only of a farm-house and two workmen's cottages, but by about 1890 it had begun to develop rapidly and now has most of the facilities of a medium-sized resort. Although dominated by two large hotels there are a couple of ordinary pubs, but they are tucked away in the side-roads and have to be sought out.

The official route follows the road for 200 yards before escaping onto sandy turf, once occupied by a short-lived golf-course, but there is a third possible route.

This is the high level path over Woolacombe Down, not marked on many maps but worth considering on a clear day because it provides a view over Baggy Point from an angle not usually seen. It involves continuing up the road to the start of the Marine Drive, where a path can be found climbing steadily up the side of Potter's Hill, given to the National Trust to mark the Silver Jubilee in 1935 by Miss Chichester of Arlington Court, thus adding to her gift of Morte Point. One should aim for the stile beside a gate, and if one pauses at the stile and glances at the horizon slightly east of north, yet another standing stone is just visible. This one is much larger than the others, in fact a natural outcrop although it appears to have been dressed.

Inevitably legends have been attached to it, best expounded in *Woolmers Gazette* by Mr W. Cotton, treasurer of the short-lived Exeter Naturalists' Club, following a field trip in 1876. Although by profession a bank manager he was also a very accomplished local historian. He suggested that the name of Mortehoe derives from the stone, where legend has it the victims of druidical rites were sacrificed. He then provided an earlier version of a much-quoted tradition:

'All those unfortunates who have allowed their independence to be destroyed by their weaker, though better halves, should go to shoulder with that stone, and if a sufficient number can be found to move it, they will be immediately restored to their proper position. It is only in comparatively recent times that the name has been attributed to the rock standing off a short distance from the promontory known as Morte Point.'

Resuming the walk over the Down, as one begins the descent a glance ahead to the field above the Putsborough Sands Hotel will reveal traces of low earth banks forming a grid — almost certainly the remains of a prehistoric field system. Before the Saxons introduced a plough able to turn the sod, cultivation was done with an ard, which merely cut a single furrow. Cross-ploughing was required for the soil to be broken up effectively and for this the land was best divided into small roughly square fields.

The descent through the gorse brings one to the official path. It is better to cross this and go down the steps by the National Trust warning notice. One can then glissade down the dunes to reach the beach, and the recommended route.

Alternatively and perhaps the best route from Woolacombe is the signposted middle course, over springy turf protected by the first sand dunes to be encountered on the walk. A wind speed of more than ten miles an hour is enough to move the grains, picking them up from the beach at low tide and depositing them wherever an obstacle, natural or artificial, slows the ground wind speed below that threshold. The most effective natural obstacles are marram and sand couch grass, fast growing so that they can keep pace with the accumulating sand, and with extensive root-systems to help bind it. The decay of these pioneer colonists provides the humus which enables other plants to establish themselves, notably some mosses and lichens, which further stabilise the surface and form the fixed or grey dunes in which a wider variety of plants can survive.

The problem is that the colonising grasses are very susceptible to damage from the trampling of holiday makers, which results in the sand being blown further inland to the annoyance of all concerned. Hence the erection of palings, both to break the wind speed and to keep the holiday-maker out, thus giving the grass a chance to recover. Such palings are now a familiar sight on most dunes from here to Sennen Cove, and while it is always presented as a temporary measure, I occasionally wonder whether free access will ever be allowed again.

The attraction for me of this section is the low-growing Burnet Rose in early summer (curiously not found on the larger Braunton Burrows) and the silver-studded blue butterflies in late summer.

After about half a mile the official path climbs to the Marine Drive, but I prefer to continue level for as long as possible before being forced down to the beach near the Black Rock, actually reddish Pickwell Down Sandstone.

There are some very desirable properties around here, one of them the home for some years of the writers Negley and Daniel Farson. Originally there was just Vention cottage, the home of a lime-burner, and the lime-kiln. The name is said, although not by the experts, to be an abbreviation of 'invention'. In support of this is quoted Risdon, writing about 1630, 'And of late, a new invention hath sprung up, and been practised amongst us, by burning of lime, and incorporating it for a season with earth, and then spread upon the arable land, hath produced a plentiful increase of all sorts of grain where formerly such never grew in any living man's memory.'

More modern properties now abut the lime-kiln, and about a hundred yards beyond it a path leads off the beach past a refreshment kiosk. From here an amenity path runs through the caravan site up to the stile. Although not a right of way I have never heard of any difficulties here. Once over the stile two large earth banks will be noticed — almost certainly lynchets associated with the ancient field system running up the slope.

> The official route from Woolacombe continues past the end
> of the Marine Drive, along a track which comes out by the
> Putsborough Sands Hotel, from where it follows the lane for
> 200 yards up to a stile. Just over a mile inland is the village of
> Georgeham, to which Henry Williamson came in 1921 after

three traumatic years in the trenches. Such an idiosyncratic writer was bound to find it difficult to gain acceptance in the close-knit community of a Devon village. However, Williamson succeeded to the extent that his fictionalised accounts of the village trying to adapt to the post-war world as recounted in *The Village Book* and *The Labouring Life* are in my view the best things he ever wrote.

The route continues more or less level above cliffs recently re-classified as Upcott Slates. Just over half a mile beyond the stile, the path descends very slightly as it enters a field with a ruined barn by the south-east corner, although this cannot be seen from the path. The next two fields appear utterly undistinguished, yet their name, Bloodhills, commemorates an alleged incident from the darkest of the Dark Ages. To quote Cotton again:

Tradition relates that when England was only known as a little island, 'butting upon the Kingdom of France, there were two chieftains — Crida, of Mercia, and Moira, who must have been in a small way about these parts. Crida was anxious to have a slive of territory in North Devon, and thought he would try his luck by a raid upon his neighbour, Moira. The latter naturally objected to this proceeding, and, summoning all his resolution and his followers, he met the enemy on Baggy Point, and utterly routed him. From this incident, it is said, the village of Croyde derives its name. I have never seen this legend in print. It was told to me — I am afraid to say how many years ago — by a local antiquary, and I cannot vouch for its accuracy.

Cotton's contemporary, J. R. Chanter, an equally accomplished local historian, provided a somewhat different version, attributing the battle to the 'naval irruptions of the Danes'.

Many are the legends along the North Devon Coast of these Corsairs. Crida and Putta, two of their chieftains, are traditionally said to give names to well-known places in Barnstaple Bay, Croyde and Putsborough, and close by are some steep downs still designated the bloody fields.

Resuming the walk, when the signpost to Middleborough Car Park is reached one is level with Wheeler's Stone, although it is only revealed at low spring tides. There is a more substantial tradition concerning this particular name. It is held that it should really by Willer's Stone, a local diminutive of William, the Christian name of one of the crew of a Braunton-owned ketch, who landed on the rock and claimed it in the name of Queen Victoria.

Soon the corner is turned and some very dramatic scenery gained. The Upcott Slates give way to Baggy Sandstones, the rock-climbing qualities of which have only fairly recently been recognised, although Page recounts a rather improbable story of a visitor to the huge cave of Baggy Hole getting trapped by the tide, 'and spent four dreadful hours climbing the cliffs, cutting notches in the shale with his pocket knife.'

Another rocket post crowns the headland, this time a more typical specimen, beyond which a sheer drop used to be known as Baggy Leap. The name may derive from another nebulous tradition related by Mr Cotton which concerns two 'fond and foolish lovers who preferred to die together rather than obey the parental command to part'. Other writers have taken it to derive from the leap of the waves.

This was the scene of the most disastrous shipwreck along the North Devon coast, that of HMS *Weasel*, stationed at Appledore and caught by a sudden north-westerly gale in February 1799. All 105 on board perished, and very few of the bodies were ever recovered.

The route now progresses south-eastwards briefly, with a view across Croyde Bay to Saunton Down, and beyond to the coast past Westward Ho! The lower path here is to be preferred. After about 500 yards the Baggy Sandstones give way to the younger Pilton Shales, transitional between the Devonian and Carboniferous, which here provide the best example yet of a raised beach, perhaps better called a wave-cut platform. These evidently result from wave-attack at a time of higher sea-level, and vary in height along the south-west coast up to about sixty feet. They can all be dated to the Pleistocene period (or Ice Age) but the problem in explaining them is that the effect of water being locked up in an ice-sheet would have been to lower the sea-level, conceivably by as much as 500 feet. Therefore these higher levels must relate to one of the interglacials, or the much briefer interstadials. There is no general agreement yet on the dates of the various heights.

After half a mile one reaches the National Trust sign by the little stream at Freshwater Gut, and a classic Mesolithic site. 'Mesolithic' describes the period when groups of hunter-gatherers occupied Britain for a period of perhaps four thousand years from the end of the Ice Age until the arrival of Neolithic farmers who brought with them techniques of making pottery and polishing stone axe-heads. Mesolithic man was dependent on flint tools, but these he exploited to their limits. Anthropological parallels suggests that hunter-gatherers lived in bands of between twenty and thirty, with about six active males. They probably made their way across what is now the North Sea before rising sea-levels made Britain an island again some eight or nine thousand years ago.

It is suggested there were only about forty such bands in Devon and Cornwall, hunting mainly red deer on the uplands in summer, and resorting to the coast in the winter in search of flint pebbles, from which were derived the carefully worked arrow-heads. There was presumably a winter camp here, when the diet would have been chiefly limpets and mussels, perhaps supplemented at more favourable times with the bark of young elm together with oysters, cockles and even salmon from the Taw and Torridge estuary.

Large numbers of discarded flint flakes have been found in the area, and even today it is possible to find the odd one or two on the path leading up the hill. They have presumably been gradually washed down from the higher ground over the last seven thousand years.

Another area where flints have been found is on Lundy, indicating that it was Mesolithic man who began our maritime tradition, probably in skin boats resembling the eskimo's umiak. While early Mesolithic man was living in harmony with his environment, he was aware of how to start a fire, and it was probably later Mesolithic man who started forest fires in order to improve hunting, thus beginning another of our traditions; that of damaging the environment to produce short-term gains.

Continuing the walk, and keeping as close to the cliff-edge as possible by the Baggy Point Hotel, a backward glance will reveal, lodged at the base of the cliff among the mesembryanthemum (also called Kaffir or Hottentot fig), the largest of several erratic boulders in the area, which are believed to have been deposited by an ice sheet during the Ice Age. Another three smaller ones, all of different materials found no nearer than Scotland, have been recorded within a hundred yards.

Soon one is forced to go inland behind some houses and a field, before reaching the beach at Croyde Bay, where there can be problems at high tide. Those in search of alcoholic refreshment must resort to the village half a mile inland. The best route is to leave the beach where the larger of the two streams loses itself in the sand, and head due east, making for the stile beside the camp toilets. There is some dispute among geomorphologists as to whether the landforms along here are more properly regarded as raised beaches or river terraces. From the stile a path leads into the village, emerging conveniently beside the Carpenters' Arms. There is an infrequent bus service, except during the peak season, through Saunton to Barnstaple.

The walk continues along the low cliffs of Sauton Downend, above another raised beach, where there are four more erratic boulders. A flower to look out for in summer is the sea stock, which is only found in these few miles of coast, and on the Glamorgan coast. It should not be confused with the hoary stock, found on the North Cornwall coast, which has deeper purple flowers and a woody stem.

A notable wreck off here was the ketch *Ceres*, built in 1811 at Salcombe, and evidently made to last. Her first duties were conveying stores to Spain for Wellington's Peninsula Campaign. She was bought by a Bude ship-owner in 1852 and lengthened a few years later. At the age of 101 she was fitted with an auxilliary engine, and survived the First World War. Twenty-five years later, having carried over a quarter of a million tons of cargoe, she sprang a leak and foundered, the crew being taken off by the Appledore lifeboat.

An irritating stretch now follows; one is forced up the road near a castellated look-out and the path resumes just above the road for about a mile. What makes it particularly irritating is that the cliff-edge path was shown on a map published by Devon County Council as recently as 1975, and it gave one an opportunity to view another erratic boulder, this time of red granite. This is now accesible only by scrambling over the rocks at low tide. The official path runs below the slope of Saunton Down, which has yielded evidence of early man from the Mesolithic period to the Bronze Age. Just before the hotel is reached the slope is cut by prominent cultivation terraces, provisionally dated to the Saxon period.

The route then passes through the grounds of the Saunton Sands Hotel, although it is apparent that the Hotel owners would rather it did not. Once down on the beach there seems to be a choice of routes, although for the true coast walker it is no choice at all.

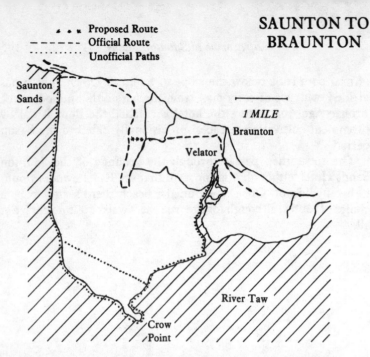

Proposed Route
Official Route
Unofficial Paths

SAUNTON TO BRAUNTON

Saunton Sands

1 MILE

Braunton

Velator

River Taw

Crow Point

SAUNTON SANDS TO BRAUNTON

Either 5¼ or 8 miles depending on the route taken

Unofficial route along the coast.   8 miles.
Recommended. At its best botanically in July

EXCEPT at high tide, it is possible to walk along the beach, which stretches for three miles beside Braunton Burrows, one of the largest dune systems in the Country.

These three miles witnessed some animated scenes in January 1843, when, to quote a local poet,

'The John and Lilley came Ashore
To feed the hungry and clothe the poor.'

The barque *John and Lilley* was fourteen days out from Liverpool bound for Calabar when heavy weather led to her hold filling with water. When her pumps and rudder failed she was driven ashore, the crew of twenty-three being saved. On the high tide she broke up and all her cargo of rum, beads, fire arms, cutlery, iron, ironmongery, copper, and bales of printed cotton were strewn along the whole length of the beach.

The reactions of the local people and the censorious editor of the *North Devon Journal* were predictable.

The officers of the revenue, customs and coastguards, were very actively engaged all day on Sunday in superintending the saving of the cargo; and it required their utmost efforts to preserve it from pillage; and but for their timely assistance and resolute defence, most of the property would have found its way across the sandhills . . . The vigilant precautions of the commanding officer of the customs were barely sufficient to deter the bands of men and women that came down from purloining and carrying away whatever they could lay their hands upon. Another tide or two and the whole of this fine vessel will have disappeared. . . . It is with indignation we record to the lasting disgrace of this neighbourhood, that the most bare-faced and shameful robberies have been committed on the wreck, and that not merely by the poor and ignorant: but by those who should have set an example of honesty to others. It is reported that one gentleman in a horse and gig left the strand laden with booty on Sunday, but we hope this is not true.

The following week the editor quoted another witness.

On Sunday all our opposite sects were merged into wreckites and never was a more busy day for man or beast. The shore was thronged with wretches, hardened as the rocks that surrounded them, wholly intent on plunder. Farmers from this and the adjoining parishes continued, through the day, to cart off whatever they could put their hands on, and the night came without causing a cessation of their unhallowed labours: and that which is most disgracefully remarkable is, that not a single member of the unpaid made his appearance to check the work of devestation.

The unpaid was a reference to the magistracy, and this criticism brought a rejoinder in the next issue from the nearest magistrate, the banker Zachary Hammett Drake, who lived six miles away: 'he was entirely uninformed of the occurrence until the day after it happened . . . if he had been apprised in time, not only would his personal services have been enlisted immediately, but the North Devon Yeomanry would have been in readiness at a few hours notice to co-operate with him.'

I could find only one report of a prosecution resulting from this, when a farmer and his labourer were found to have on their cart over a hundredweight of tobacco. At the trial, the bench found themselves unable to accept the claim of a number of witnesses that there had been no tobacco on the cart until the coastguard had thrown a bundle on it. They found the case proved, and imposed fines of £100, which I believe was then mandatory. As the labourer was unable to pay such a sum, it being about four times his annual income he was sent to prison for a year.

To resume the walk along the strand-line; a few plants manage to survive in this hostile environment, notably sea rocket and the less attractive prickly saltwort and frosted orache, dependent on nutrients from the decaying seaweeds, and under constant threat from exceptionally high tides. The dunes nearest the beach are likely to be stabilised by sand couch grass, which is more salt-tolerant than marram.

After about a mile the Burrows incongruously combine the functions of a Military Training Area and a National Nature Reserve. About half a mile further on, and now lost beneath the sand, was the site of the Appledore Number Two lifeboat station. When conditions were so bad that the Appledore boat could not get over Bideford Bar, the crew would row across the estuary while local farmers provided horses to drag the boat into the surf. Drifting sand meant that the station had to be moved inland three times, but during the period that it functioned, from 1848 to 1919, eighty-five lives were saved.

A further half-mile brings one to the end of the military training area by the J lane, built by American troops training for the Normandy landings in the Second World War, but now just another track through the dunes. The Nature Reserve continues south of the track, and there is unrestricted access on foot to some of the best botanising England can provide.

> My own inclination is to forsake the beach here, heading south-east roughly in the direction of the chimneys of West Yelland Power Station. To ecologists the interest of a dune system is that the natural succession of plant communities, established over a period of time, can in this case be observed on the ground. As one walks more or less in the direction to

which the prevailing wind is blowing, one traverses progressively older dunes with more mature vegetation. In this case the prevailing winds are from a few degrees south of west. They also bring in minute shell fragments, which make the area attractive to lime-loving plants.

Initially, the low foredunes are colonised by sand couch grass. Then come the larger dunes in the process of being stabilised by marram, but supporting a few other plants such as sea spurge and the more attractive sea holly and sea bindweed. As one moves eastwards over the fixed dunes, the water table comes closer to the surface and the valleys or 'slacks' between the dunes can be permanently moist and colonised by creeping willow and marsh pennywort.

The particular glory of the Burrows must surely be these dune slacks, where in June the brick-red variety of the early marsh orchid can be found, but even more rewarding is July, with the marsh helleborine and round-leaved wintergreen. The latter first appeared during the 1950s and has spread vigorously since. It seems destined to replace the water germander, which was locally abundant when the last County flora was published in 1939, but is now confined to one small patch, and that threatened by the invasive sea buckthorn.

According to my hundred years old copy of *Flowers of the Field* the water germander was at that time used as a tonic by rustic practitioners! Today it could prove a very expensive tonic for it is one of the sixty-one rarities fully protected under Schedule 8 of the Wildlife and Countryside Act. Any rustic practitioner found to have even part of the plant in his possession would be liable to a fine of up £500 for each plant.

Other flowers to be found are yellow bartsia and yellow-wort, blue fleabane, Portland spurge, houndstongue, pyramidal and southern marsh orchids, clustered club-rush (first recorded here in 1662 by John Ray, the founding father of British natural history), and the diminutive French or sand toadflax, which has spread across from Northam burrows where it was introduced. More careful searching will be needed to find autumn gentian and the strange little ferns, moonwort and adder's tongue.

A word of warning may not be out of place here; Braunton Burrows are big enough to get lost in. Here, on a misty day many years ago I learnt to my intense adolescent chagrin that

I was not immune from the tendency to walk round in circles.
But aiming for the power station chimneys should bring one
out close to the car park at Broad Sands, where in July the
pale yellow of the evening primroses and the deep blue of the
viper's bugloss provide a colour contrast unsurpassed anywhere else along the 560 miles of path.

Those who find botany uninspiring can continue along the
shore, with the Fairway bell buoy a nautical mile out beyond the
low water mark to indicate the approach to Bideford bar. This
provides only a few feet of water at low tide, causing John Leland,
Henry VIII's librarian, to observe 'The Haven entry is barrid with
sande and the enterie into it is dangerous.' More than 300 years
later a report to the Admiralty observed 'the loss of life and
property in the bay exceeds (for the space) that of any other portion
of the coast of the United Kingdom'.

Inspite of this a large maritime community grew up around the
Rivers Taw and Torridge. At one time as many as 120 ships would
sail out over the bar on one tide, but little remains today of the
traditions of the Barmen. The largest cargo was limestone from
South Wales. As much as 90,000 tons a year were shipped over the
bar destined for the forty kilns built on the banks of the Two
Rivers. Up to 60,000 tons of sand and gravel were shipped out.

The limestone trade gave rise to controversy during the 1840s.
According to the 1847 Admiralty report, 'The baneful practice of
casting limestone heaps promiscuously upon the otherwise navigable
margins of these waters ... and to leave it until it suits the
convenience of the adjoining landowner to cart it away ... besides
presenting reefs of sunken stones six and eight feet high for vessels
to hang upon in the track which ought to be clear for evolution,
causes an addition of loose hard matter to the usual river deposit.'

It was claimed that these man-made reefs had caused the loss
of a 200 ton merchant vessel, an Admiralty yacht, and a Coastguard
revenue cutter. Another practice in the trade was to have the heavy
work of unloading done by womenfolk, who would heave the
stones up from the hold for the men to drop overboard.

At Airy Point a slight change of direction brings Appledore into
view. A few hundred yards further on, Old Wall Rocks on the edge

of the tideway hints at some lost archaeological feature. Another 500 yards brings one to what was once the site of the low light which in Page's day was a mere box, mounted on a tramroad, on which it is moved to and fro, according as the bar shifts its position. For the two lighthouses must be brought into one by vessels making for the estuary.'

The upper light stood 300 yards beyond. This was a conventional lighthouse, except that it was on the roof of a substantial house, built in 1822. At the time of the *John and Lilley* wreck the keeper's name was, most appropriately, Mr Lampin. The survivors were brought here to dry out, in more than one sense, since some of them had got at the rum.

The lighthouse was demolished in 1957 and replaced with a lattice-work structure, but it remains immortalised in Charles Kingsley's 'The Three Fishers' written in 1851:

> Three wives sat up in the lighthouse tower,
> And they trimmed the lamps as the sun went down;
> They looked at the squall, and they looked at the shower,
> And the night-rack came rolling up ragged and brown.
> But men must work, and women must weep,
> Though storms be sudden, and waters deep,
> And the harbour bar be moaning.

The girder tower has recently been demolished (most inconsiderately, because the only way I could find the water germander site was by lining the tower up with the village of Instow) and a new lighthouse erected on the promontory of Crow Point.

Years ago, ketches would beach along here to load sand and gravel, which was taken across the channel for the South Wales building industry. Most of the docks from Swansea along to Avonmouth were constructed with aggregate from this area. At the time of writing, just one barge continues the tradition, negotiating the maze of coastal protection regulations, to supply Barnstaple.

At the base of the sandy cliffs the yellow horned poppy can be found, with seed pods up to a foot long. The salt marsh at Broad Sands is less botanically inspiring. Here glasswort functions as the pioneer colonist, trapping the silt so that the level of the marsh begins to rise. This means that it is covered by water for shorter periods, and therefore becomes accessible to less salt-tolerant species such as sea purslane and annual sea-blite.

The next landmark on the walk is The White House which was originally the Ferry House. In Page's day the Appledore ferry would row across when required, but today's coast walker has to make a long diversion to bridge the Taw and Torridge.

Some half-mile west of The White House was the site of St Ann's Chapel. *Murray's Handbook* for 1850 refers to the ruins, but they were later lost under the sand. There is the vaguest of traditions that there was also a village there.

The walk is best continued along the top of the embankment which protects Horsey Island. Although this is a right of way, it is almost invariably overgrown. Inland can be seen the two-mile long embankment (with the toll road beside it) dating from 1815, when the marshes were drained in a controversial scheme planned by the Exeter engineer James Green (best remembered today for the Bude Canal) using the techniques pioneered in Holland. The draining of the land resulted in some of the best cattle-raising pastures in the county.

The more seaward embankment dates from the 1850s and was engineered by Nicholas Whitley, a Cornish surveyor with geological and antiquarian interests. He was a man willing to learn from nature, and modelled the slope of the embankment on that of the pebble ridge at Westward Ho! He used the same sized pebbles, locally known as 'popples', which now provide a home for some of the more attractive salt marsh flora; sea lavender, two of the sea spurreys and the September-flowering sea wormwood.

Features of the inland scene are the straight stone hedges and now ruinous linhays which provided shelter and shade for cattle. Some were surrounded by stone pounds, which could be plugged to provide a refuge in the event of the dyke being breached. The last major breach was in 1910.

At Pill's Mouth the route turns north. The presence of RAF Chivenor can hardly be ignored. When the jetty is reached one is level with the main runway, and the jet training planes using it seem to be literally a few feet overhead.

Just beyond, the original embankment comes in, and another 300 yards brings one to the Toll House, built originally for the marsh inspector. Here begins the new cut, constructed in 1860 to enable ships of up to 200 tons to reach Velator, the port of Braunton. Over to the right can be seen the original winding course of the River Caen.

After 400 yards one reaches Marstage Farm, which was on the edge of the Great Field. The Tithe Map of 1841 shows that between here and Kiln Cottages there were sixteen different strips averaging less than twenty-two yards across which were worked by twelve different cultivators. Little evidence of strip cultivation remains today.

Nor does much remain of Braunton's contribution to this island's maritime history, although a modest but significant chapter of that story was written here. The fitting of sailing vessels with auxiliary engines was pioneered at Braunton and survived longer here than anywhere else. Braunton-owned and crewed schooners and ketches carried gravel and farm produce across to South Wales, returning originally with limestone but later coal which they continued to import up until the 1950s. Today nothing remains apart from a few photographs and the memories of the older inhabitants. Braunton men were known in the other Bar ports for their custom of taking their bicycles to sea with them. This served the very practical purpose of enabling them to cycle home when windbound in a neighbouring port, to work their plots on the Great Field.

There was a dispute here in 1931 over the right of mooring. This came about when the landowner built a corrugated iron shed over one particular mooring post. One of the owner-skippers took exception to this, and procuring an axe, smashed a hole in the side before an enthusiastic crowd, thus enabling him to moor his boat in the accustomed place. At the ensuing court hearing his action was upheld, the judge taking the view that the shed formed an obstruction to established moorings and rights of loading and unloading.

From here the route continues over Velator Bridge, past industrial and commercial premises to pick up the old railway line, where one turns right for Barnstaple.

SAUNTON SANDS TO BRAUNTON

Official Route. Currently 5¼ miles; when fully open 3½ miles
Not Recommended

THIS is the shortest route to Braunton and should be considered only by those in a hurry. For many years it has provided a depressing example of the casual attitude, if not outright contempt, of officialdom in this country towards the pedestrian.

The path runs along the beach for perhaps fifty yards before passing through the car park, and follows the access road for some 200 yards before forking right along a narrow track, potentially overgrown. At one point Star of Bethlehem has escaped from a garden. The road has then to be followed for a quarter mile before one turns into a lane just past the golf course entrance. From here the route runs south-east for half a mile, partly across the golf course, before turning south through the scrub on the edge of the course.

In high summer some will find this stretch pleasant enough, among the melilot and meadowsweet, but the latter is an indicator of damp conditions, and the path can be under water in the winter. Some fifty yards beyond a public bridleway signpost there will be noticed on the left a barbed wire fence. The more optimistic walkers will scrutinise it closely in the hope of finding a stile here. The official route, approved by one Environment Minister in 1961 and formally opened by another in 1978, involves the creation of 500 yards of public footpath through a single field to Sandy Lane Farm, thus saving the walker a diversion of nearly two miles.

Although the latest edition of the Ordnance Survey's 'Pathfinder' map shows the path to be open, on my last visit there was no sign of either a stile or any work in progress. The hardened South West Way walker realises that the time-scale involved in the creation of a footpath can be vastly longer than that for a six-lane motorway.

As it is, the winter walker must continue his aquatic progress southward. Once through the second gate one is in the Nature Reserve and Military Training Area. Some 600 yards beyond, keeping to the 'temporary diversion', a ruined building will be noticed on the edge of the field to the left. This was the old Burrow House, a reminder of the times when the Burrows were a huge commercial rabbit warren, producing 2,000 rabbits a day.

Shortly after passing the Burrow House one turns left to reach Sandy Lane Car Park. From here the path runs northwards along roads that, most unusually for Devon, run straight. These were produced by the rulers of the enclosure commissioners early in the last century when the marshlands were drained.

Sandy Lane Farm was once a bulb farm but is now a gas-bottling plant. Here one turns right along Moor Lane to reach Swanpool Bridge and the new wooden stile just beyond it. Once over this stile one follows beside the hedge for 150 yards until another new wooden stile is reached. From here the official path turns east-north-east along a right of way that heads directly to where a hedge ends abruptly. The trouble is that for many years now there has not been a vestige of a trace of such a path on the ground. Many walkers will feel happier going round the edge of the field, although this is technically a trespass, rather than proceeding directly over the cabbages, or potatoes, or wheat.

Having reached the end of the hedge, one can pause to survey the Great Field. This is, or perhaps was, one of the three best survivals of medieval strip cultivation in the country. The 365 acres were divided into some eighteen blocks, known as 'shotts' or 'furlongs', and demarcated by 'bond' stones sunk in the ground at the corners. These furlongs were then divided into strips, separated by grassy banks, originally turned up by the plough. They were known locally as 'balks' or 'landsherds'.

Ownership of the strips was once divided, seemingly randomly, among three manors: Braunton Abbots, Braunton Gorges and Saunton, and were then further divided among the tenant cultivators. The last major survey, in 1889, showed that there were 491 strips worked by fifty-six cultivators. Incidentally this was at a time when it was the fashion among the more cloistered agricultural historians to claim that there had never been any true open field system in Devon.

Virtually the only change over the next fifty years was that the strips tended to come onto the market and be eagerly snapped up by local farmers. In 1939 the Air Ministry announced its intention of constructing an aerodrome on the Great Field, but it encountered so much flak from conservationists, in the shape of letters to *The Times*, that it was forced to turn its attention to Chivenor.

Damage to the Field in the post-war period has been more insidious. Consolidation of the strips and modern agricultural techniques have led to a gradual ploughing out of a substantial number of the balks. A County Council report in 1982 suggested that about thirty per cent of the strips remain, but in my view a figure of ten per cent would be closer to the mark, and I do not know of a single bond stone remaining. On my last visit the entire north-west quarter had been converted to sheep pasture and enclosed behind a wire fence.

The official path follows this fence eastwards, with chicory in flower in high summer, to reach the broad path across the Field at a point where there are actually six balks intact. Here one can get something of a picture of what is also called the Midland system of cultivation, although examples of such sub-divided fields are now known to have occurred in every English county. The system was originally thought to have been introduced by Saxon settlers, but is now believed to have evolved during later Saxon times. Questions as to how and why it came to replace the earlier system of 'Celtic' fields, and when it reached its maximum extent, have yet to be resolved.

In 1305, Edward I decreed that a standard acre was to be 220 yards long and 22 yards wide, the length being known as a furrow long or furlong, and was the length that could be ploughed by a team of eight oxen without needing a rest. The acre was the area that could be ploughed in a normal day. In the Great Field there are some differences from the typical Midlands system. These particular strips are only 200 yards long, while a comparison with the Tithe Map of 1841 shows that there were then ten strips, varying in area from less than a half to one and a quarter acres, so even here there has been some consolidation. Other differences are that the strips in the Midlands are believed to have been separated by deep furrows and not balks, and that the slightly curving shape, enabling the plough-team to be more easily turned onto the headland at the end, is absent here.

To resume the walk, one follows along the broad path for some two hundred yards, to a point where it veers very slightly to the left. Here it is necessary for me to record that there exists a difference of opinion as to the ministerially-approved route. Devon County Council take the view that it continues up the path and presumably out into the main road. In stark contrast, the view of the Countryside Commission and the Ordnance Survey is that the path branches off to the right towards the brick pill-box that guards the cricket field. For many years there was no trace of the path on the ground but on my last visit a new path was visible that more or less followed the line on the map.

A few years ago I was sufficiently exasperated to complain that the only indication of the right of way was a public footpath sign by the road as the far end. Even that had disappeared by my next visit.

The 1982 Report by the County Planning Department did draw attention to the problems facing the walker and proposed the improvement of the path network, but it is not so many years ago that another department at County Hall 'improved' my local bus service by providing less buses. With the County Council dominated by farmers and landowners it remains to be seen whose interpretation of an improvement will prevail.

Having negotiated the stile by the brick pillar-box, one skirts the boundary of the cricket pitch before crossing the road and proceeding along Mile Stile. This brings one to the hump-backed bridge over the River Caen, with domestic ducks usually in evidence. Just beyond, the presence of railway lines embedded in the road provides evidence of the erstwhile Barnstaple to Ilfracombe line, and by turning right along Station Road one passes an incongruously sited railway signal to arrive at the stile marking the start of the path along the line into Barnstaple.

The problems of negotiating the Great Field could drive many people to drink, and the presence of the award-winning Mariner's Arms may be of interest some two hundred yards away in South Street. There are some photographs in the bar commemorating Braunton's vanished maritime tradition. More relics are to be seen in the little museum that opens for a few hours a day in the summer. This is next to the church at the top end of the village, which claims to be the largest in England.

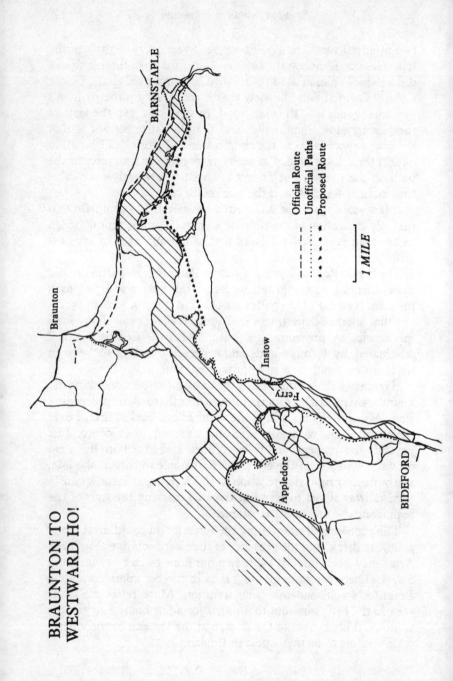

BRAUNTON TO
WESTWARD HO!

BARNSTAPLE

Braunton

Instow

Ferry

Appledore

BIDEFORD

Official Route
Unofficial Paths
Proposed Route

1 MILE

BRAUNTON TO WESTWARD HO!

17 miles via the Instow to Appledore ferry, which runs only during the four summer months and is even then subject to tides

THIS section is more estuarine than coastal and is not very inspiring. At the moment there is no official path between Barnstaple and Westward Ho! Those anxious to resume cliff walking can make use of the frequent bus service from Braunton through Barnstaple, Instow and Bideford, with alternate buses terminating at Appledore and Westward Ho!

BRAUNTON TO BARNSTAPLE   5½ *Miles*
Official route along the old railway line

THE stile at the end of Station Road gives access to the old railway track from Ilfracombe, which closed in 1970. This became a right of way in 1981, and although a gravel surface is not everyone's idea of a coastal footpath it is now part of the official path. Initially it follows beside the River Caen for 500 yards until the road from Velator Quay is reached. At this point those who have followed the unofficial route around Crow Point rejoin the path.

A further hundred yards brings one to the parish of Heanton Punchardon, with the church visible on the hill to the left. Edward Capern was buried in the churchyard. He is worth a mention in a book about walking because he enjoyed some modest acclaim in the middle of the last century as a postman-poet. His first employment was in a Tiverton lace factory, where at the age of eight he was required to work a shift of up to twenty hours. Having survived this he eventually became a postman at Bideford, which involved walking to and from the village of Buckland Brewer, five miles away. On his walks verses would come to him, which he would later write down. These verses were not about exploitation, but about celandines and violets, except during the Crimean War when he relapsed into jingoism (not that the word was coined until the next attempt to pick a fight with Russia over

119

the Eastern Question in mid-century) with 'The Lion Flag of England', with which the Prime Minister, Lord Palmerston, was much taken.

Once past the old Wrafton station house one comes to RAF Chivenor. The original airstrip was built in 1934, when for fifteen shillings return the Lundy Air Line would convey one to the island. With the coming of the Second World War Chivenor was requisitioned and extended to enable it to play a significant role in the Battle of the Atlantic. The crew of one German bomber mistook the Bristol Channel for the English Channel, landed, and were taken prisoner.

With the return to peacetime conditions Chivenor became a training unit until this was transferred to Pembrokeshire in 1974. Only the rescue helicopters remained, and peace descended on the estuary. It proved to be a short-lived peace, however, for by 1980 the RAF were back in force, although bird-strikes remain a perennial problem, and occasionally the odd kamikaze seagull manages to write off a few million pounds' worth of aircraft.

The estuary is reached just before Heanton Court, now a free house. The next three miles provides moderately good bird-watching in autumn and winter. Sea clover, sometimes very aptly called teasel-headed clover, has been recorded along here, but I know it only from the Instow side. Once past the Pottington Industrial Estate one reaches the rugby ground, where it is necessary to fork left (unsignposted on my last visit), then right into Mill Road, passing through somewhat down-at-heel surroundings to emerge by the Rolle Quay Inn, which is a good place to stop for a meal.

One feature of interest in Barnstaple is the Castle Mound, prominent opposite the Civic Centre. Entirely artificial, it was constructed within fifty years of the Norman Conquest. The path takes one and a half revolutions to spiral up it, although small boys manage the direct ascent. There are a couple of benches on the grassy plat among the butchers broom, but the mature beeches restrict the view.

The Pannier Market is also worth a visit on Tuesdays and Fridays, but it is so crowded that it is no place to be with a backpack. The St Anne's Chapel Museum is behind Butcher's

Row, while the North Devon Athenaeum, by the Long Bridge, has another museum with a good collection of local minerals, fossils and artefacts.

BARNSTAPLE TO INSTOW

For the seasonal ferry

7 miles, if the old railway track is followed

BARNSTAPLE is left by the Long Bridge over the River Taw. Conservationists regret the replacement of the ornate Victorian wrought iron lamp standards by the characterless modern examples. It has recently been suggested that there was originally a bridge here in Saxon times and that it was constructed to deny the Viking long boats access to the higher reaches of the river. This would have been a most ambitious project for the period, and it is likely to be a long time before such a conjecture is accepted.

Once over the bridge one turns right along a path that runs through the middle of a furniture factory. One then passes heaps of gravel and the employees' car park to emerge on Anchor Wood Bank, above the saltings.

After 600 yards one arrives at the old railway line from Barnstaple to Bideford, and a choice of route. The railway closed to passengers in 1965 and to freight services in 1982. Despite the efforts of preservationists who were hoping the line might one day be re-opened, the track is being removed at the time of writing. Almost certainly the route will become in due course a further section of the South West Way, and those genuine walkers who follow the route before it officially becomes a right of way are unlikely to be challenged. It certainly provides the shortest route to Instow.

The line runs virtually straight for over a mile and a half before entering a cutting, the sides of which are of considerable interest to geologists. The cutting reveals pebbly clay and sand which has been derived from the boulder clay that covers the lower ground away to the left. This must have been deposited by an ice sheet, and provides the only tangible evidence that the glaciation reached as far south as Devon. The deposition is believed to date from the Wolstonian stage, the penultimate advance of the ice sheet, and since some of the boulders are believed to come from Ireland it seems that the whole Irish Sea was covered.

The episode has provided some economic benefit to the area. The ice front was stationary near Fremington long enough for a river to be dammed by it, and a lake formed. In this lake were deposited fine muds, free from boulders, which have proved suitable for use as potter's clay. This has been quarried at several points south of the main road.

Fremington pottery was highly regarded in Cornwall during the last century, and shiploads of ovens and pilchard pots were regularly dispatched from Muddlebridge, at the head of Fremington Pill. The quite bizarre method of counting in the industry suggests that it must have been of some considerable antiquity: a 'sea' dozen comprised sixty items, while a 'land' dozen was a mere thirty-nine. About a hundred years ago the industry switched to smaller, more artistic products and it still survives to this day.

One emerges from the cutting at what was Fremington Station by the mouth of Fremington Pill. This was once a hive of activity. Not so long ago it was the second busiest port in the county. Before nationalisation the Southern Railway imported its coal from South Wales here, while ball clay from Peter's Marland, twelve miles to the south in a part of Devon well off all the tourist routes, was shipped out. There are also several very substantial lime-kilns.

Another straight stretch of track follows. After just over a mile the fields to the right give way to saltings. The more recent maps show the Yelland stone row in the mud a few hundred yards north of here, but it is visible only at low spring tides. It is regarded as either late Neolithic or early Bronze Age, and indicates that the sea level must have risen significantly over the last four thousand years.

After progressing some 500 yards nearer to the disused West Yelland power station, a bank will be noticed on the right. At this point a right of way starts abruptly which allows one to follow the shore all the way to Instow. This is the only place where I have managed to find sea clover.

Beyond the power station and level with Crow Point is the Instow Fish Bed, which derives its name from the coelacanth fossils that it yielded around the turn of the century; this also is accessible only at low spring tides. On the dunes just before reaching Instow is to be found the perennial wall rocket.

> Those who have reservations about walking along what is not a right of way must follow the path under the railway line at Anchor Wood Bank and along to the dripping well. This was once believed to possess curative properties and is now covered in liverworts. The path through Anchor Wood is then followed and at the end one passes through a kissing gate into the Oakland Park Estate. By turning right into Lynhurst Road and then left into Oakland Park South, and then taking the third turning on the right one arrives at a footpath. This leads to a T-junction and by turning left here and then immediately right one arrives at a stile leading into a field.
>
> A glance over to the right reveals the ruined Ellerslie look-out. From the top of the octagonal structure pilots could watch for ships approaching the Bar.
>
> The walk is continued downhill beside the hedge to arrive at a farmyard, where one turns left into a lane which brings one out onto the main road at Bickington. From here it is four miles to Instow and a further three on to Bideford. As substantial stretches are without a pavement it is well worth re-considering the idea of taking a bus.

BIDEFORD TO APPLEDORE   *2½ miles*
Unofficial extension of the path, recommended only when the ferry is not operating

BIDEFORD gives the appearance of being a prosperous market town, dominated by its bridge, which is said to date from 1280 although it has been widened and repaired on numerous occasions since. There is now very little activity around the tree-lined quay, and the days when Bideford was the fifth largest port in England have long gone. There are associations with both Sir Walter Raleigh and Sir Richard Grenville. The port was well placed to benefit from the trade in dried cod from Newfoundland, Britain's first colony, and later from the tobacco trade with Virginia, until that transferred to Bristol around 1750. Much of the architecture facing the quay, and particularly along Bridgeland Street running down to it, reflects those more prosperous days.

The statue of Charles Kingsley repays the debt owed to him by Bideford for his favourable mention of 'the little white town which slopes upwards from its broad tide river paved with yellow sands', at the very start of his best-selling *Westward Ho!*, which was written during the Crimean War at Northdown House, a quarter mile away and now a convent school. Kingsley was a supremely talented man, an enthusiastic geologist and naturalist, with the gift of conveying his enthusiasm. It is a little ironic that he should be remembered principally for this jingoistic book that delighted a country raised to fever heat over what some claim to have a been a totally unnecessary war.

The walk continues past Victoria Park, with its allegedly Armada cannon, and just beyond the defunct Bideford Shipyard turns inland along a narrow lane before re-emerging on the shore at Cleave Houses, at the bottom of Limer's Lane. As well as a lime-kiln, this was the site of a celebrated shipbuilding yard in the days of sail. In fact this whole path used once to be called the shipwright's path.

Another short diversion follows before returning to the shore. A recent breach of the dyke has necessitated a detour through the field, just before the Bidna yard of Appledore Shipbuilders. This was the largest covered yard in Europe when it was opened in 1970, and has been one of very few industrial success stories in North Devon, enabling Appledore's shipbuilding traditions, which stretch back more than 200 years, to be continued. From here the road has to be followed into Appledore.

Just above the quarry stood Chanter's Folly from 1841 until it was demolished in 1957. Hardly a folly, it served the very practical purpose of providing a view out over the bar and enabling the approach of any of the ships owned by Thomas Chanter, a local magnate, to be signalled to his Bideford office.

Then comes what used to be the New Quay Dry Dock, which was owned by P. K. Harris, a famous firm of wooden shipbuilders who survived the inter-war slump only by cutting profit margins to nothing. It was a tradition for many years that at each launching ceremony the hymn, 'Lead, kindly Light' would be sung. During the war several wooden minesweepers were built, but the firm was forced into liquidation in 1963. This in turn led to the formation of Appledore Shipbuilders.

Beyond the bend in the road was once Benson's New Quay, built about 1745 by Thomas Benson, who for a brief period managed to combine the roles of entrepreneur, Member of Parliament for Barnstaple, and villain. His undoing occurred in 1752 when he bought a very old ship, the *Nightingale*, loaded her with cargo and convicts for the Colonies, and insured her heavily. He then unloaded the cargo and convicts on Lundy Island, which he had leased, sank the ship, and claimed the insurance money. Eventually the story of the plot leaked out, necessitating the speedy departure of the Honourable Member before he could be apprehended to an exile in Portugal. The captain of his ship was less quick off the mark; he failed to escape and at the age of twenty-seven his career was abruptly terminated before a lively crowd at Execution Dock in 1754.

At the junction with Myrtle Street is the Richmond Dry Dock, built by the autocratic William Yeo about 1856. It takes its name from Richmond Bay on Prince Edward's Isle off Nova Scotia, which was largely settled from the Bideford area. The shipbuilding and timber trades on the island were established by William Yeo's father.

Just up Myrtle Street is Odun Road, which commemorates Odun, Earl of Devon, who according to tradition defeated Hubba the Dane near here, although Countisbury has much the better claim. Odun Road houses the North Devon Maritime Museum, open on summer afternoons and well worth a visit. Here are preserved what remains of the local traditions, although the schooner *Kathleen and May* which worked out of Appledore until 1960 has been preserved at Greenwich by the Maritime Trust.

The walk continues past Docton House, said to be fourteenth century, to the Quay, which was widened during the last war to provide a Marine Parade. Here the ferry passengers from Instow are landed.

APPLEDORE TO WESTWARD HO!
Unofficial extention of the path.   4½ *miles*

APPLEDORE can make no claim to being a holiday resort of long-standing. To quote a writer in *John Bull* back in 1868, 'The inhabitants are as wild and uncivilised a set as any to be found in this part of the kingdom and where, till lately, a stranger could not pass without insult.' Even today, Bideford people still occasionally speak of Appledore as the place where they ate the missionaries.

A feature of the quay is the number of 'opes' leading off it. 'Ope' is good Devonian for a narrow passage way leading off a waterfront. A more general term is 'drang', and there is one of those at the end of Market Street. Beyond the parish church, built in 1837, one comes to Irsha Street, which interrupts the view of the estuary. Nevertheless, it contains some rather attractive houses, a few of them seventeenth century. Many of them were occupied by master mariners during Appledore's heyday.

At the end of the street is the Customs House, although this was originally by the Richmond Dock. Just below it is the lifeboat house. The first Appledore lifeboat was established in 1825, the year after the founding of the RNLI, at a site to the west of the present station. In 1922 the first motor lifeboat to serve the Bristol Channel was housed here. Over the years, and including the Braunton Burrows station, some 500 lives have been saved.

The walk can be continued close to the shore to reach Hinks' yard, where the tradition of wooden boat building still survives. Here were built the replicas of the *Nonsuch*, to mark the Hudson Bay Company's tercentenary, and the *Golden Hind*, used in Drake's four hundredth centenary circumnavigation.

At low tide one can progress seaward of the yard, and over the little bridge to Northam Burrows, which tries to combine the disparate roles of Country Park and rubbish tip. No doubt the latter will one day be landscaped but for the present one should not expect too much. One can proceed along the shore past some very botanically uninspiring salt marsh and around to the point, where the sea holly provides some attraction.

Inland is the Royal North Devon Golf Club, founded by the

local vicar in about 1860, after his cousin from St Andrews had observed that Providence evidently intended the Burrows for a golf links. It was only the third course to be constructed south of the Tweed. The Royal title derives from the patronage of the Prince of Wales in 1867, but the course is best known for its association with J. H. Taylor. Taylor was brought up in modest circumstances in the village of Northam, and took to caddying at the Royal North Devon to earn pocket money. He went on to become the first Englishman to win the Open Championship, at the age of twenty-four. He died in Northam in 1963 aged ninety-one.

Near what became the seventh green was situated for some fifty years the Northam Burrows lifeboat station. As with the Braunton station, horses from a local farm were used to launch the boat into the surf. There is a very good story, although it strains credulity to its limits, that when the horses heard the maroon go off they would jump over the hedge and make their own way to the station. For brief periods during the last century Appledore had three separate lifeboat stations.

At high tide it is a mile and a half trudge over the pebble ridge into Westward Ho! The ridge is very vulnerable during westerly gales. A breach was made as recently as 1975, hence the current protection scheme involving filling gabions with the pebbles to increase stability. The custom of 'pot-wallopers' assembling on Whit Monday to throw the pebbles back onto the ridge was discontinued much longer ago than most guidebooks would have one believe. Another effect of the storms has been to pivot the ridge about a point some one-third of the way along so that it faces more directly westward, by perhaps five degrees over the last 150 years. The effect has been to cause severe erosion at Westward Ho!, necessitating the building of a sea-wall in the 1920s.

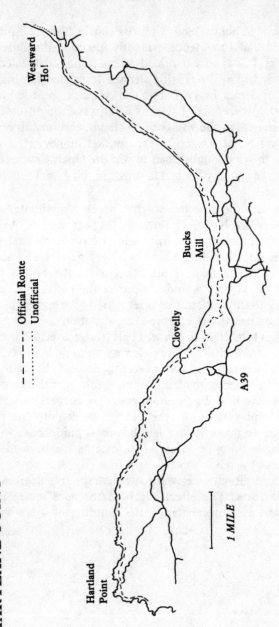

WESTWARD HO!
TO
HARTLAND POINT

Westward Ho!

Bucks Mill

Clovelly

A39

Hartland Point

- - - - Official Route
.... Unofficial

1 MILE

WESTWARD HO! TO HARTLAND POINT

Best in May when the bluebells are out
18 miles

UNLIKE virtually every other community met with along the coast, the origins of Westward Ho! can be accurately dated, in fact to 1863 when a consortium of local businessmen formed a public company intended to develop the area into a resort to rival Ilfracombe. To quote from the prospectus of the Northam Burrows Hotel and Villas Company:

This Company has been formed for the erection of a Family Hotel, on an estate purchased for the purpose immediately contiguous to Northam Burrows, and of Villas and Lodging Houses for Sale or Lease. The want of such accommodation has long been felt, and as no attempt to supply it has hitherto been made by individuals, it is deemed to be a legitimate project to be undertaken by a Company. . . .

The Hotels and Villas will be situate . . . close to the Burrows — a wide expanse of smooth turf, 1000 acres in all adapted for cricketing and the Scotch game of Golf, and protected from the sea by the extraordinary pebble ridge — with a noble beach of hard dry sand, two miles in extent, fitted for equestrian and pedestrian exercises.

Very prudently, the prospectus continued:

With regard to the expected dividend, the directors will not follow the usual example of holding out unreasonable expectations. Having shown that the undertaking will afford a legitimate supply of a long felt want, they think themselves entitled upon the principle of demand and supply, as well as from the experience of other projects of a kindred nature, to anticipate a fair and reasonable return for the capital expended.

The following year, according to the owner of the *Bideford Gazette*, 'a happy idea struck Dr Ackland, one of the Directorate, to christen the new settlement Westward Ho!' Kingsley was not happy with the idea. In a much quoted letter that year to Dr Ackland, he wrote 'How goes on the Northam Burrows scheme for spoiling that beautiful place with hotels and villas? . . . men

129

like me must look out for a new planet to live in, without fear of railways and villas projections.'

Kingsley is not widely regarded as a conservationist, and yet he was one of the first Englishmen to begin the thankless task of trying to popularise the radically new doctrine originated by the American ecologist George Perkins Marsh. In 1871 Kingsley accepted the Presidency of the Devonshire Association, which had among its membership five directors of the Company. In the course of his Presidential address he developed his theme: 'And we who, with all our boasted scientific mastery over Nature, are, from a merely mechanical and carnal point of view, no more than a race of minute parasitic animals burrowing in the fair earth's skin, had better, instead of boasting of our empire over Nature, take care lest we do not become parasites too troublesome to Nature ... in which case Nature, so far from allowing us to abolish her, will by her inexorable laws abolish us.' His views were to fall on deaf ears for the next hundred years.

1871 was also a year of some significance in the history of Westward Ho! Following the success of the professional Prussian Army over the French, pressures for reforms in the British Army became irresistible. In that year the purchase of commissions was abolished and a competitive examination for Woolwich and Sandhurst substituted. This led to the formation of a company which aimed to set up a school with a syllabus geared directly towards the Army examinations. It was to be an alternative to the more expensive traditional public schools with their bias towards the classics.

The failure of Westward Ho! to develop as fast as the promoters had anticipated meant that property with space for playing fields was available at a bargain price, and so in September 1874 the United Services College opened under the headmastership of Cormell Price, in what had been a terrace of twelve lodging houses.

The real Cormell Price was not a particularly headmasterly figure. He had been at school with Edward Burne-Jones and at Oxford with William Morris, and retained his contacts with the pre-Raphaelites for the rest of his life. His main qualification for the post was that he was a superb teacher. It was thus appropriate that Burne-Jones' nephew Kipling, J. R., should have been sent to the school run by his 'Uncle Crom' while his parents were in India.

This is not widely realised that the account of Kipling's school-days revealed in *Stalky & Co* is a work of considerable imagination; parts of it are in fact a travesty of the truth. For instance, Price is depicted as an authoritarian figure aiming to turn out a stereo-typed product anxious to die for his country. In January 1878, the very month that Kipling arrived, with the jingoes clamouring for another war with Russia, the real Cormell Price was in London helping to organise anti-war meetings.

Another distortion of more relevance to coast-walkers is to be found in the very first chapter, in which the boys are trespassing on the cliffs in defiance of the notice-boards threatening prosecution, erected by the peppery Colonel Dabney, JP. According to a golf historian, he was in real life Captain G. M. F. Molesworth, RN, JP, a prominent member of the development company and shown by the directories to have been living in the very urban surroundings of Northdown Hall at Bideford during the four years that Kipling was present. The guidebooks of that period recommend the invigorating walk over the cliffs to Clovelly. Only after 1905 when the Judiciary gave the go-ahead to the path-stopper did the notice-boards appear, and they stayed up until 1978.

For those who believe facts are more interesting than fiction, even Major-General L. G. Dunsterville's own account, in *Stalky's Reminiscences* is suspect. He attributes the closure of the school not to Price's failure to control the boys, but to his failure to control the staff. Actually, the school was moved nearer to London in 1904, ten years after Price had retired to Sussex. The most reliable record was given by the third of the trio, M'Turk, actually G. C. Beresford in his *Schooldays with Kipling*, and it is well worth searching out.

The school was the more easterly of the two blocks of Victorian terraces, and has recently been converted into flats. A memorial window to Cormell Price, together with the school's Roll of Honour, can be seen in the church.

The block to the west, built of the rather sickly local yellow brick, was also a school for a brief period. It was founded in 1882 as the Kingsley Memorial College for educating 'the sons of Noblemen and Gentlemen on Sound Church of England Principles', but it lasted less than four years, and the block is now holiday flats.

The walk resumes along the promenade, which in 1939 was the scene of a battle to prevent the establishment of a holiday camp, the first in the county. Having lost that battle, the amenity groups seem to have lost all further interest in the war against despoliation. Westward Ho! has become a mass resort with all the amusements and services that this implies, and not the slightest attempt has been made to plan in harmony with its once fine surroundings. It is the sort of place the coast-walker hurries away from, consoled by the thought that there is nothing else like it for another hundred miles.

The earliest visitors to Westward Ho! were Mesolithic people, and they were not particularly tidy either, having left the remains of numerous meals in the shape of a kitchen midden site, accessible only at the very lowest spring tides. Over the years it got covered with blue clay and peat, but careful examination has revealed many worked flints, together with the shells of oyster, limpet, mussel and winkle to provide evidence of the diet. The presence of bones of red and fallow deer, as well as wild boar, proved that more substantial meals were also enjoyed.

The interest of the site to the experts is that the peat covering has been radiocarbon dated to give an age of around 5,500 BC. By assuming that the site was originally just above high water mark, a figure for the rate of rise of the sea level over the period of between thirteen and twenty feet has been obtained.

In view of our enthusiasm for burning up fossil fuels, which increases the level of carbon dioxide, and leads via the 'greenhouse effect' to further melting of the ice caps, the rise seems destined to continue, with consequences not too difficult to predict.

Continuing the westward progress, above a prominent raised beach, the last house is close to the site of a pier that was nearly 500 feet long and took nearly three years to build in the 1870s. The sea took far less time to demolish it. The pillars are said to be still visible at the lowest tides.

It was along this next stretch that the ceremony for the official opening of the South West Way was performed by Denis Howell,

MP. It took place in May 1978, although the path was not yet completely open to walkers at that date.

The path continues below Kipling Tors, a gorse-clad hill given to the National Trust by the Rudyard Kipling Memorial Fund two years after his death in 1936. At Rock Nose direction changes to south-west and one is forced up to join the track bed of the short-lived Bideford, Westward Ho! and Appledore Railway, a standard gauge concern that opened in 1901 and just managed to survive until 1917 when it was requisitioned by the Government and shipped over to France, to the relief of the directors. Just over half a mile further on the track swings inland, and some real coast-walking resumes. The path now follows cliffs composed of Carboniferous sandstones and shales, which make up the cliffs now for virtually the whole way to Boscastle. The whole sweep of Bideford Bay is now revealed, with a view past Bucks Mills and Clovelly to end at Hartland Point.

At low tide ribs of rock are revealed running out for some 300 yards. These are known locally as rames or ranes, words also used to describe bony remnants or a skeleton. The six-inch map labels one particular spot, nearly 200 yards out, as Fanny Bennett, apparently referring to a conical rock, more or less covered at high tide. While I have no information as to why this seemingly unremarkable rock should be so named, I am not totally devoid of information on the subject of a Fanny Bennett who resided in this parish of Abbotsham. An Exeter newspaper for September 5th, 1835, contained a paragraph concerning a lady of that name living in the village, just over a mile inland. One of her hives was invaded by a swarm of strange bees, and thinking to smoke them out she procured a lighted torch. But it had been a hot, dry August and she was insufficiently careful with her torch, with the the result that within an hour her cottage was completely gutted.

Passing on to less irrelevant matters, there is a gentle descent to the old lime-kiln, where a path from the village provides access to the shore. Even here there are 200 yards of ranes to be negotiated before a vessel could lie 'sewed', to discharge its cargo of culm and limestone. Sewed is another local word meaning left dry on the beach by the recession of the tide.

From here, a gentle climb for some half-mile brings one up to a stile in a stone-faced hedge, with disturbed gorse-covered ground on the other side. Unless I am much mistaken this was the site of a coal mine. This is the only place I know of where this Carboniferous rock lives up to its name, a narrow band of anthracite running due east for some fifteen miles. However, the combustible quality of the anthracite was so poor that it was more valued as a pigment called 'Bideford Black'. The mining was presumably open cast, and yet there is what appears to be a very narrow adit down on the beach. A couple of hundred yards brings one to the ruin of Greencliff lime-kiln, which, uniquely, was fired by home-produced coal.

After a few more hundred yards one reaches Boatlake, lake being an old word for stream, which has here cut a little ravine to divide the parishes of Abbotsham and Alwington. Just beyond is the site of the wreck of the *Eva V*, a Cypriot coaster which drifted ashore in March 1981 when the tow line parted, while she was being towed to a scrapyard. Within a week she had been stripped of everything movable by persons unknown. They still like to keep up the old traditions around here.

A steady climb up through a mass of gorse brings one to the summit of Cockington Cliff, beyond which one descends, passing what looks like a disused mine-shaft, right down to the beach. Those who form the opinion that there is more up-and-down work along here than is strictly necessary are quite correct; an intended bridge across the ravine was abandoned in an economy drive.

From the beach one has to slog up Westacott Cliff before negotiating the broken slopes of Babbacombe Cliff, with a few late blooms of musk mallow among the scrub to provide a welcome show of colour on my last visit. Eventually one emerges onto open cliff at Higher Rowden, with a good view forward.

Just ahead are the red cliffs between Portledge and Peppercombe, an isolated outlier of the same Permian sandstone as the South Devon cliffs, familiar to countless thousands of holidaymakers, and laid down under desert conditions around 250 million years ago. Beyond lie six miles of tree-covered slopes beginning with the crag of Peppercombe Castle and ending in the almost sheer face of Gallantry Bower. This part of the bay is sheltered from the salt-laden westerly gales, enabling more prolific vegetation to become established.

One descends to Portledge Mouth, and the little stream running down from the Portledge Hotel, previously the home of generations of the Coffin family, almost back to the Conquest. From here it is half a mile, which can be taken along the shore at low tide, to the stream at Peppercombe which marks the boundary with Parkham parish. The earlier six-inch map marks a point just on the Alwington side of the stream as Giffard's Jump, commemorating a local legend that is typical of the genre in that it exists in more than one contrasting version.

The best known is the one consisting of thirty-three somewhat tedious verses, which relate how Thomas Giffard, heir to a local estate, was married at Parkham Church (this has been dated to 1537 by surviving documents), after which the bridal party repaired to the cliffs to partake of refection. Honeymoons are a more recent innovation.

> '"Come forth my love," the bridegroom said,
> "Come look upon the Severn Sea,
> Yon cliff that proudly lifts his head
> Shall be a seat for you and me."'

No doubt with her mind on other things, the bride gets too near the edge and loses her balance. In attempting to save her, successfully, Thomas himself loses his balance and disappears over the edge. The bride is taken home prostrate with grief, but there is a happy ending; she recovers on hearing his voice. His fall had been broken by

> '. . . a ragged oak
> That half way down the cliff had grown.'

From there

> 'A jutting stone, a gadding briar,
> Were aids upon my perilous way'

enabling him to

> '. . . the lower cliff ascend
> And hasten to his happy home.'

And thus

> 'Ages have pass'd and names are gone,
> But living still in local lore —
> Right well the "Giffard's Leap" is known
> To those who tread that rocky shore.'

In Polwhele's version, which has the decided merit of being briefer, and which he dates to around 1740, a youth on a party of pleasure managed to fall over the 130 foot cliff 'yet received no manner of hurt.'

A stile by a copper beech leads one over the stream, beyond which another stile marks the start of the wooded stretch, at its best in May when the bluebells are out. One climbs steadily up to the field, and into it for a short distance. To the casual observer this is a perfectly ordinary field, but it is actually part of Peppercombe Castle, which is believed to be an Iron Age promontory fort. At the top corner there is a massive bank down to the next field. A much smaller curving bank and ditch cuts off a small area near the path, but what with the scrub cover and two thousand years of erosion, it is difficult to make sense of the site.

The path continues through Sloo Wood for threequarters of a mile until at Gauter Pool, which has gone the same way as virtually every other pond in Southern England, there is a sharp left turn and a climb up to Worthygate. From here the ridge is followed, and just before descending steeply down under the trees, a gap in the hedge to the right discloses a gorse-covered bank. This is the eastern end of what is presumed to be another promontory fort, with an extremely steep slope to the north, but there is uncertainty as to whether it dates from the Iron Age or Dark Age.

The descent into Bucks Mills takes one past a modern coastguard look-out, from which one gleans the information that the auxiliary coastguard is called Braund. The path emerges into the village opposite Grenville Braund's seasonal shop, which provides pots of tea for thirsty walkers. One is thus disposed to accept the tradition that at one time all the inhabitants were Braunds, although it must date to a period well before census returns. Another tradition is that they all descended from the survivors of a Spanish Armada galleon.

To quote from a nineteenth century journalist, 'The Braunds have a decidedly foreign appearance and those who pass members of the family on the road are forcibly struck by their distinctive type of complexion and feature. Captain James Braund, the King of Bucks Mills, can many a tale unfold of notable incidents in the history of his tribe.'

Another journalist was less impressed with the patriarch: 'a corpulent individual with the gift of the gab.'

Captain Braund was in the habit of reciting a poem of thirty-six verses, extolling the virtues of the men of Bucks, while accompanying himself on the fiddle. The verses were published as a broadsheet by a Bideford printing firm, and perhaps it is worth quoting a few of them:

> The Braunds of Bucks! the Braunds of Bucks!
> A race of hardy Men!
> So full of courage, that their 'pluck' —
> Eternally remain.
>
> FIVE GENERATIONS OF THIS RACE —
> Have not yet passed away;
> All born at Bucks, a rocky place,
> In Bideford's snug Bay.
>
> Renown'd as Fishermen of old,
> So they continue now,
> And launch their Boats like lions bold,
> To guide each fishing Plough.
>
> No Haven have they! not a Pier!
> Wherein to moor their Craft,
> But up and down the rocks, with care,
> They haul them fore and aft.

Four verses then deal with the economy of the village:

> Mountains and rocks surround each home,
> Whereon their goats do feed,
> Supplying heather for the broom,
> And kids and milk in need.

Advent'rous Braunds! Advent'rous Braunds!
They launch into the sea;
They 'cast their nets', their wives catch prawns,
While they mesh fish with glee.

Now hauling in their silver prey,
Perhaps a dozen meas;
And home they come without delay,
And shake them out like bees.

Oh! what a gladsome — glorious sight,
These Mack'rel and the Herring!
A gift of God! view'd with delight, —
By wives and children cheering.

The remainder of the verses deal with the heroic efforts of James.

JAMES' Life Boat is a Herring Yawl
A little open Prow:
Has weather'd many a storm and squall,
And SAVED TWELVE LIVES we know.

The word 'meas', pronounced 'maize' around here, might well puzzle some readers. It is a unit of herrings, which varied around the coast of Britain from 500 to 630 fish. Sir Frederick Pollock, referred to in the introduction, was sufficiently intrigued to write to *Notes and Queries* in 1874 to seek enlightenment, but without success:

At Clovelly, Bucks, Bideford, Ilfracombe, and as far as Lynton, herrings are sold by the 'maze' or 'meas' of 612 fish. This number is arrived at in the following way: the herrings are counted by the handful of three fish, called a 'cast'; and thus, when forty casts have been counted, 120 fish have been reckoned, equal to a 'long hundred'; ten more casts are counted, and the number reached by the addition of these thirty more fish is 150. Then the fisherman calls out "cast", and throws in another cast, completing the number to 153 fish. This process, repeated three times, gives the number of 612 fish ...

The custom is a very old one, and no explanation of its origin, or of the meaning of the word 'maze' or 'meas' seems to be known. 'Cast' probably means the same as 'throw' — as many fish, that is, as can be conveniently thrown or handled at once. The number 153, of course, recalls the number of fish in the miraculous draught of fishes; but this suggestion, when offered, is a novelty to the fishermen of Clovelly and Bucks; . . . the coincidence may, probably, be only accidental, curious as it is . . .

The village has changed little in appearance over the years, and it is well worth while going down to the beach. King James' boasting was firmly grounded in fact — to have successfully launched boats from such an exposed beach for generations dic' require seamanship of a very high order, perhaps surpassed only on the West Coast of Ireland. The only protection was from the ridge of rocks running northward for some 350 yards, called the Gore, but this is awash at half tide. The earlier six-inch maps mark Old Quay Point just inside it, presumably that referred to by Risdon as having been erected by Richard Cole, who is said to have died in 1614. There is no trace of a quay there today. By the turn of the century there were only sixteen herring boats left, built at Appledore and carvel-built in order to withstand the stresses from the pebbles, but numbers gradually dwindled to nothing.

Two legends worth recounting are that the Gore was an attempt by the Devil to construct a causeway to Lundy, which he was forced to abandon when he broke his shovel, and that Richard Cole was the original 'Old King Cole'.

The most prominent features of the beach are the lime-kilns, one a splendid castellated structure with an inclined plane up which the lime would be drawn by a horse gin. A channel was cut through the reefs, known as the Gut, to enable the stone hackers bringing limestone from Caldy Island to beach closer to the kiln.

On a more cultural note, J. M. W. Turner found his way here in 1811: 'a good pedestrian, capable of roughing it in any mode the occasion might demand'. He sketched an animated scene around the smaller kilns, with Clovelly in the background. Bucks Mills features briefly as Beera Mills in *The Wages of Sin* by Lucas Malet, the pseudonym of Charles Kingsley's daughter Mary, not to be confused with her cousin Mary, the African explorer. Many of the Victorian critics thought the book to be daring and unpleasant.

The only depressing feature of the village is that three-quarters of the cottages are now holiday lets, and thus deserted most of the year, effectively destroying any chance of preserving the village as a community.

Another divisive element is the stream, which separates the parishes of Parkham and Woolfardisworthy. The latter must cause headaches for the Post Office — there is another parish of that name in mid-Devon. It was also an even older boundary, dividing the Saxon Hundreds of Shebbear and Hartland. The problem of the origin of the Hundreds remains one of the most intractable of Anglo-Saxon history, indeed exactly what they were hundreds of has yet to be clarified. One version suggests that they were formed democratically by a coming together of local freeholders once a month, meeting in the open air at some prominent spot to discuss and reach decisions on local matters concerning law and administration. The moot-place could even be an archaeological site; Dorset had a hundred of Culliford Tree, one of a group of barrows. Alternatively, they could have been imposed from the top, as convenient units for regal revenue raising purposes.

It has been suggested that they follow even older boundaries, stretching back to the misty Celtic past, perhaps to when the land of this country was first parcelled out, and research into this subject bridging archaeology and documentary history is currently fashionable. Hundreds declined in importance after the medieval period and were superseded by district councils at the end of the last century.

As the hundredal boundary can hardly have been drawn through the middle of a community, it seems probable that there was no Bucks Mills in late Saxon times. This is borne out in the Domesday survey, which lists the manor of Bochiwyis, which must be Bucks Cross, up on the main road, and entirely within Woolfardisworthy parish. While fisheries are mentioned in Devon, these are confined to the estuaries and presumably involved fishing weirs. Sea fishing seems at that time to have been restricted to East Anglia. The picture regarding water-mills also suggests that the South West was the less progressive part of England. Although known to the

Romans, the Domesday picture strongly suggests that water-mills spread out from the South-East of England, and by 1086 had reached only as far as East Devon. To sum up, the origins of this, the first genuine fishing village encountered on the walk, should be sought in the less well documented later Middle Ages.

The path out of Bucks Mills climbs up through the wood, soon coming to a fork. While the path to the right would lead one to a view of Heritage coastline, officialdom has decreed that the walker must take the left fork, which shortly provides a view of a holiday camp, albeit an up-market one. Having regained the fields again, one soon discovers that the Heritage Coast is marred by assorted old cars and fertiliser bags. Beyond, one continues in the shade cast by mature beech trees and then through a couple more fields to cross over a stream into Clovelly parish and the Hobby Drive.

It is customary for guide-book writers to go into ecstasies over the Hobby Drive, but I have to express my dissent. The two principal things I expect; views of coastal scenery and freedom from motor traffic; are largely lacking. While there are brief glimpses of the coast between the trees, in season they are likely to be monopolised by motorists. Yet I know of only one writer who shares my views, a *Western Morning News* journalist who wrote in 1950 of 'the quietness now shattered by the roar of passing motors that compels pedestrians to be quick or dead.'

For all that is written about the Drive in the guide-books, its origin remains obscure. It is said to have been the hobby of the second baronet, Sir James Hamlyn-Williams, who inherited the estate in 1811 and died in 1829. There's uncertainty as to whether the actual work was carried out by French prisoners of war, or whether it was to provide winter relief for the Clovelly fishermen during the post-war depression. A further source of confusion is that for the sixty-six years that the baronetcy existed all three baronets were called Sir James.

The Hobby Drive provides a more or less level shaded walk of nearly three miles, contouring round the combes. After three-quarters of a mile there is a gentle climb along a newer section cut in 1901 after landslips had closed part of the original stretch. Following this, one contours round the two streams whose waters join to fall into the bay at Freshwater 400 yards east of the pier. A tiny stream is then crossed. This used to flow down Clovelly High Street until diverted behind the houses in the eighteen-sixties. A further 300 yards brings one to the top of the cobbled street.

Actually the official path continues straight on, but I have never heard of anyone who resisted the temptation to turn down the street. As Arthur H. Norway wrote in the *Highways and Byways* volume, 'one is the richer in experience for having seen Clovelly; elsewhere there is nothing like it.'

It was first popularised by Charles Kingsley, whose father was rector here for four years, in a series of essays on North Devon published in *Fraser's Magazine* in 1849. Its popularity became such that by 1883 the pressure of visitors arriving on the steamers from Ilfracombe was having an adverse effect. To quote from a writer in the *Pall Mall Gazette*: 'There is much provision for the tourist and the visitor; but there is very little trace indeed of the true-born aboriginal hardy fisherman. ... The Clovelly of today is just a tourist's masquerade of a fishing village. ... Gateways bar all the approaches; it is 4d here, 6d there, a shilling yonder, till the unhappy amateur begins to reflect that this is not exactly the untutored wilderness to which he was looking forward.'

In fairness it has to be said that the tolls went towards local charities, of which Clovelly had been in dire need, but the degeneration was abruptly reversed the following year when Christine Hamlyn became mistress of Clovelly on the death of her elder brother, and began a reign that was to last fifty-two years.

She was a formidable conservationist. Although only five feet tall she was of sufficient stature to take on the potential developers and leave them utterly vanquished. Even in her seventies she would patrol the street, dressed in severely Victorian style, and on sighting an unregulated garden, or less than tidy dustbin, would give her tenant the benefit of her opinion on the matter. Her death at the age of eighty was the occasion for genuine mourning by 'her people'. Her best memorial must be the number of cottages bearing the letters 'C.H.', indicating that they were faithfully restored during her reign.

The Estate Company has continued to follow her precepts,

and while it is fashionable to deride such land-holding as a relic of feudalism, the only alternative is a free market that would destroy Clovelly as a community even more effectively than it has destroyed Bucks Mills.

As one descends over the cobbles, to the left is Mount Pleasant, given by Christine Hamyln to the National Trust in memory of those who fell in the Great War. The High Street must surely be the only one in the kingdom that has never seen wheeled traffic. Everything from the beer kegs for the New Inn to colour televisions for the inhabitants has to be dragged down the cobbled steps on sledges. As Charlotte Chanter, sister of Charles Kingsley, and wife of the vicar of Ilfracombe observed, 'Anyone who ventures down Clovelly street must leave his dignity behind him, and get down as best he may, fortunate if he have not a hard tumble or two by the way.' Countless thousands do take the risk.

Perhaps half a dozen of the cottages provide bed and breakfast, and outside July and August it should be possible to find a room. As the ground floor of one cottage tends to be level with the chimney of the next there is a good chance of a view across the bay. Additionally, the best time to see the village is early and late in the day, without the tidal wave of engulfing humanity. Much has been written about the avariciousness of the locals at intervals over the past hundred years, but my experience has been that the prices are, if anything, slightly lower than those in larger resorts.

One continues down past the New Inn (which I am able to recommend), past the strategically sited Doctor's surgery, and past the look-out, with its antique barometer and RNLI collecting box. There is a seat here which makes a good spot to pause on the way back. The route then goes under Temple Bar where a house is built over the street, and so down to Quay Pool, dominated by the Red Lion, where the beer and everything else arrives by land-rover down the back road.

The original pier was built about 1600, when the Carys were Lords of the Manor, and enabled Clovelly to become the centre of the herring fishery. In 1837 a Harbour of Refuge was proposed. This would have been achieved by building a massive breakwater out from Mouth Mill, but without Government support the scheme was prohibitively expensive.

Over the years Clovelly has seen more than its share of tragedy. The worst was in 1821 when twenty-four boats were lost during a tremendous gale, drowning thirty-one fishermen and leaving nineteen widows and sixty-one children destitute. A relief fund was set up and nearly £3,000 raised. In 1838, when Charles Kingsley was at Cambridge University, disaster struck again, with another twenty-one drowned. He later wrote of the second tragedy

... the bay darkened with the grey columns of waterspouts, stalking across the waves before the northern gale; and the tiny herring-boats fleeing from their nets right for the breakers, hoping more mercy even from those iron walls of rock than from the pitiless howling waste of spray behind them; and that merry beach beside the town covered with shrieking women and old men casting themselves on the pebbles in fruitless agonies of prayer, as corpse after corpse swept up at the feet of wife and child, till dawn saw upwards of sixty widows and orphans weeping over those who had gone out the night before in the fullness of strength and courage. Hardly an old playmate of mine, but is drowned and gone ...

His 'Three Fishers' was evidently based on first-hand experience. One particularly unnecessary calumny of the local people is to be found in the Reverend Baring-Gould's biography of Parson Hawker:

... the vicar of Morwenstow in a claret-coloured coat, with long tails flying in the gale, blue knitted jersey and pilot boots, his long silver locks fluttering about his head ... was appealing to the fishemen and sailors of Clovelly, to put out in their lifeboat to rescue the crew of the *Margaret Quayle*. The men stood sulky, lounging about with folded arms, or hands in their pockets, and sou'westers slouched over their brows. The women were screaming at the tops of their voices that they would not have their husbands and sons and sweethearts enticed away to risk their lives to save wrecked men. Above the clamour of their shrill tongues, and the sough of the wind, rose the roar of the vicar's voice; he was convulsed with indignation, and poured forth the most sacred appeals to their compassion for drowning sailors. ... But all appeals were in vain.

The truth of the matter is very different. Hawker was possessed of a very powerful imagination, and he never believed in letting the facts spoil a good story. In fact nothing he himself wrote should be accepted without independent corroboration. Baring-Gould, who must have got hold of this account at second or third hand, wrote the book in so much of a hurry to forestall a competitor that he did not have time to check his facts. This led to his being threatened with a libel action over another distortion. Had he checked the *North Devon Journal* for December 9th, 1863, he would have found the following account: 'Two herring boats put to sea, to reach if possible, the ship and take off the crew, but, having shipped two seas, they had to abandon the attempt and put back again.' Eventually the *Margaret Quayle*'s crew were able to row ashore unaided.

It was not until seven years later that Clovelly was provided with a lifeboat, and the high regard in which the village is held by the RNLI can be seen from the fact that it was the first of only two stations to be equipped with the new seventy foot Clyde class of cruising lifeboat, which has to be moored off-shore, and has a range of nearly a thousand miles.

To rejoin the path, the quickest route is to turn off to the right just above the surgery, up North Hill and Backstairs. In all the best villages one may be uncertain whether one is on a footpath or in somebody's garden. So many flowers have escaped from the gardens to line the path; pencilled cranesbill, columbine and little robin, that some confusion is understandable. The steps lead up to Mount Pleasant and to the road, near the gate into the grounds of Clovelly Court, through which the official route runs as a permissive path.

After the first few hundred yards one should keep as close as possible to the cliffs. Just after the kissing gate a path among the rhododendrons leads one to the Cabin, a summerhouse providing a good view through the trees. The path then returns to the field for a few hundred more yards to arrive at the tall kissing gate which gives access to the deer park. There are no park deer here any more, but wild roe deer may sometimes be seen.

After another quarter of a mile one comes to the 'Angels Wings', a seat with a shingled roof supported by very eleborate carving, believed to be the work of the second Sir James' butler. The seat is also said to have been positioned here to enable the baronet to look across to Youlston, above Barnstaple, where his youngest daughter Charlotte lived after her marriage in 1819 to Sir Arthur Chichester. She died tragically young, leaving six children.

Continuing onward, Page can be quoted again. 'We emerge from the oaks and reach a heathery common sloping upwards towards a headland, the summit crowned by a handful of windswept trees. Sheer to the boulder beach, smooth and regular as a wall, falls the cliff the most perpendicular in Devon. .... The cliff is called Gallantry Bower — why, no one knows, unless, as someone suggests, the name is a corruption (like many other words in this district) of some Celtic words, and stands for *Col an veor*, the great ridge.'

Kingsley's explanation was more romantic. He attributed it to 'The Norman squire, who, as tradition says, kept his fair lady in the old watchtower, on the highest point of the White Cliff ... now a mere ring of turf-covered stones ...'

The descent from here is fairly steep and at the bottom the official path takes the broad track to the left. However, those with time to spare should certainly continue up the gentle slope of what the older maps mark as the Wilderness, to the two viewpoints. To quote once more from Charlotte Chanter, 'Here in one spot you will find a grotto hewn out of the rock, and look down at the waves, — such an awful giddy depth beneath that those most accustomed to such scenes recoil from the precipice. .... Further on is a cottage, with a verandah in front, from which we see another varied and lovely scene. Opposite are woods clothing a steep hill; on the left two woody glens, with their accompanying brawling brooks, and on the right the rocky sea-beaten shore.'

Today the grotto is known as Miss Woodall's seat, after a local lady who was evidently less prone to vertigo. The cottage was a summerhouse built originally for Lady Diana, the wife of the second baronet, and has been restored twice. From here a precipitous path drops down to Mouth Mill, and the wisest course is to retrace one's steps back to the official path.

Mouth Mill was adequately described by Kingsley in 1849,

and he provided a glimpse of the rural economy of the time. 'A deep crack in wooded hills, an old mill half buried in rocks and flowers over which wild boys and bare-footed girls were driving their ponies with panniers full of sand, and as they rattled back to the beach for a fresh load, standing upright on the backs of their steeds, with one foot in each pannier, at full trot over rocks and stones where a landsman would find it difficult to walk on his own legs.'

The privilege of taking away sea-sand, valued for the shell particles which would neutralise acid soils, from below high water mark, was given to all persons resident in Devon and Cornwall by a statute dating back to 1609. It may be of interest to quote the preamble.

Whereas the sea-sand, by long-trial and experience, hath been found to be very profitable for the bettering of the land, and especially for the increase of corn and tillage within the counties of Devon and Cornwall, when the most part of the inhabitants have not commonly used any other manure for the bettering of their arable grounds and pastures, notwithstanding divers having lands adjoining the sea-coast there, have of late interrupted the bargemen and such others as have used their free-wills and pleasures to fetch the said sea-sand, to take the same under the full sea-mark as they have heretofore used to do, unless they make a composition with them at such rates as they themselves set down, though they have very small or no loss thereby, to the great decay and hindrance of husbandry and tillage within the said counties.

The older large-scale maps often mark tracks up from beaches as sandways or sanding roads, indeed some were constructed expressly for that purpose. The Act remained in force right up to the passing of the post-war Coast Protection Act.

The dominant feature of Mouth Mill is Black Church rock, recently discovered by the climbing fraternity, with, to quote Kingsley again, 'the white sand of Braunton and the red cliffs of Portledge shining through its two vast arches . . .', although his viewpoint is not readily apparent. An unusual feature is the lime-kiln, which is protected by a loopholed wall with a firing step, used by the Home Guard, in the Second World War.

An extremely controversial wreck occurred four miles off here in December 1909. A particularly heavy sea washed away a ventilator from the 4,000-ton Sunderland steamer *Thistlemoor*, flooding her forehold and raising the propellors out of the water. Throughout the night she put up distress rockets, two of which were seen by the coastguard at Peppercombe, who tried to phone Clovelly but found the phone to be out of order. It was left to a fisherman to call out the lifeboat, which got to the scene some forty-five minutes too late, although another steamer managed to pick up nine of the crew of thirty.

Patrolling by the coastguard had been discontinued in 1903, because of the dangerous nature of the cliffs at night. This reduction in coastguard numbers led to many complaints that the system of coast watching was inadequate. The survivors of the *Thistlemoor* wreck now claimed that signals had been sent up for six and a half hours, and this was the last straw.

The local view was expressed particularly forcibly by the Coroner.

They might just as well carry a box of sulphur matches on board as carry these signals if no notice was to be taken of them. The sailors did not send up these rockets like a Crystal Palace for their own amusement, but to save lives. ... If the coastguard were out, he could not conceive how they could have failed to see these continuous flares or rockets. Whether they were so busy looking for smugglers who never appeared he did not know, but it was the answer he always got as to the duties of the coastguard. ... He supposed nothing would be done until some of the Board of Trade themselves were drowned.

With pressure mounting a demand was made for a Royal Commission into coast watching, but this was refused. The Board of Trade Inquiry into the sinking was held at Bideford the following May. At this Counsel for the Board pointed out that 'the coastguard were employed by the Admiralty and the Admiralty only, their main work was to prevent smuggling and give notice in the case of any danger in time of invasion.' This was amplified by the coastguard Divisional Officer, whose men were 'under no obligation to render assistance to vessels in distress — what the Admiralty undertook as a benevolent duty had come to be erroneously regarded as an obligation.'

The matter was taken up in Parliament by the Member for North Somerset, who harried the President of the Board of Trade at every opportunity — 'coast watching has been a shuttlecock between the Board of Trade and the Board of Admiralty ... there is no recognised authority to see that our coasts are watched for signals of distress.'

The President was sympathetic, but without Treasury sanction no extra commitments could be accepted. At the end of 1911 Treasury sanction was given to erect and staff sixty-three huts for coast watching, but the Great War intervened, when the coast-guard were drafted into the Navy, and their coast watching role was taken over by the Army and Sea Scouts.

To resume the walk; once across the stream one is in the huge Hartland parish. Here there is 'a difficult climb through a coppice of low weather-beaten oak, under the branches of which you sometimes have to creep on all fours', as Page described it. Thereafter it goes up to the National Trust sign on Brownsham Cliff, remarkably a National Land Fund acquisition. A more coastal route is in prospect, but for the present one follows through fields above the steep valley side before dropping down through drifts of bluebells, in May, to the little bridge over the Beckland Water. The Devon Trust for Nature Conservation have a nature trail around here, and it is best to follow the signposted 'Alternative Woodland Path'. This takes one as close as possible to the sheer cliffs, although the waterfall cannot be seen, before climbing up through the broom to Windbury Head, another presumably Iron Age promontory fort, but the earthworks are covered by scrub.

Another 500 yards brings one to a little dell, very attractive in early summer when the foxgloves are out. The next stretch is much used by the casual walker, being fairly level, but the presence of a hedge cuts off most of the views of the cliffs, and I rate it a rather uninspiring section.

Kingsley came this way wreck-hunting:

... in the roaring December morning ... we watched from the Hartland Cliffs a great barque, which came drifting and rolling in before the western gale, while we followed her up the coast, parsons and sportsmen, farmers and preventive men, with the Manby's mortar lumbering behind us in a cart, through stone gaps and track-ways, from headland to headland. — The maddening excitement of expectation as she ran wildly towards the cliffs at our feet, and then sheered off inexplicably; ... [Eventually, near Mouth Mill] she rushed frantically in upon those huge rocks below us, leaping great banks of slate at the blow of each breaker, tearing off masses of ironstone which lie there to this day to tell the tale, till she drove up high and dry against the cliff, and lay, like an enormous stranded whale, grinding and crashing herself to pieces against the walls of her adamantine cage.

Manby's mortar was a device for getting a line to a ship before the rocket was evolved. It was never very successful. There is one in the coastguard museum at Brixham.

Continuing westward, through pasture for a mile, one reaches the triangulation point above Chapman Rock. After a few more hundred yards the tower of Hartland Church can be glimpsed. This is the highest in Devon. A further mile brings one to Eldern Point, with a view across the sandy Shipload Bay, where the National Trust have recently cut a new zigzag path following erosion of the original one.

Beyond, the path runs beside fields divided by massive hedges, up to eight feet high, the typical 'Devon banks' of earth faced with stone. They are perhaps a thousand years old, but impossible to date, because the salt-laden winds severely restrict the plant growth; certainly there is not a tree for every hundred years. I have particularly good reason to remember these hedges, because this short stretch was opened subsequently to the official opening ceremony, which I naively assumed meant that the path was open throughout its length. Consequently I spent a good deal of time and energy trying to find a way round or over or through the eight foot high obstacles.

From here one arrives at the site of the RAF Hartland radar station, established to monitor the firing range beyond Lundy. The seaward path was constructed at the instigation of the South West Way Association. While it is a very scenic route, it is perhaps wise to keep an eye on the ground, where there are still plenty of gorse roots left to trip the unwary.

The route brings one to Hartland Point, with a seasonal

refreshment hut by the car park, a coastguard station and lighthouse, and the most dramatic change of scenery to be experienced on the South West Way.

The view was best described by Sir Leslie Stephen in 1878 when he was the editor of the *Cornhill Magazine*.

You are at a height of some hundreds of feet above the sharp ledges, foam-fringed even in quiet weather. Three-fourths of the whole circle of the horizon is occupied by sea. From your advanced outpost you look east and south along vast ranges of cliff, where headland succeeds headland in interminable series, sinking into vagueness in the extreme distance. A few seabirds are hovering and screaming in mid-air, and perhaps a passing raven just croaks out an appropriate sentiment as he floats past. Far away, the sail of a solitary fishing boat suggests the dangers of the inhospitable coast. And then, looking out seawards, you see vast shining levels gradually melting into broad shadows, and the shadows succeeded by more distant breadths of light, until at last the eye is carried to the remote band of haze, of which you cannot say whether it is sky or ocean. Inevitably you fall into the mood of the old discoverers, who, when the world was not yet mapped and measured, must have had strange dreams on such promontories of mysterious lands placed far away beyond the sunset.

... As we see the huge wave, which has come to the assault some thousands of miles, gather itself together, gleam out as if lighted from within with the brilliant blue of the pure ocean, and then bound up the rocky escarpment to fall back upon its successor, we are conscious witnesses of the eternal strife lasting from the dim geological ages which shaped continents and determines the course of our petty history.

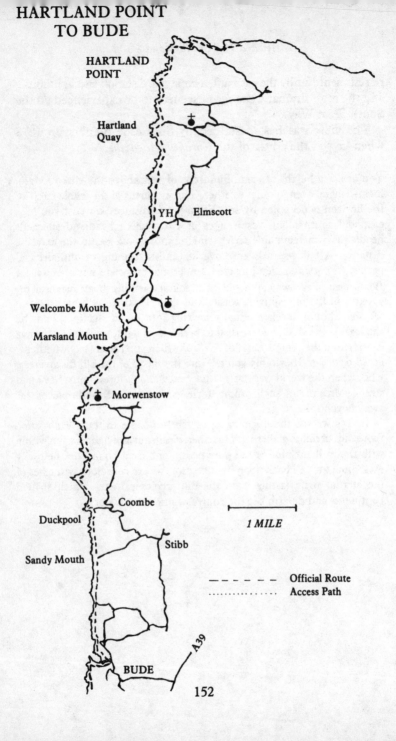

HARTLAND POINT
TO BUDE

HARTLAND
POINT

Hartland
Quay

YH   Elmscott

Welcombe Mouth

Marsland Mouth

Morwenstow

Coombe

Duckpool

Stibb

Sandy Mouth

1 MILE

– – – – –   Official Route
. . . .   Access Path

A39

BUDE

152

HARTLAND POINT TO BUDE

Perhaps best in June   *15½ miles*

ALTHOUGH Part 1 of this Guide ends at Bude, I must refer
now to a section that extends further West. Between Hartland
Point and Port Isaac are forty-five miles of what must be the
toughest walking to be found on any official long-distance path in
England. The high cliffs are cut by numerous steep-sided valleys,
which after the first few have been climbed seem to me as steep as
the sides of houses. Yet to many hardy walkers this is the best
part of the 560 miles. Certainly it provides an unforgettable walk,
but it depends so much on good weather for its enjoyment that I
have to admit a preference for the balmier southern shores. Bad
weather along such an exposed stretch can turn the walk into a
survival course, and bus services parallel with the coast are
virtually non-existent. Only Hartland Town has a service, and
that infrequent, via Clovelly into Bideford.

The lighthouse at Hartland Point was opened in 1874,
construction having taken three years. Such an inaccessible site
had to be surveyed from the sea before the road was blasted out of
the side of the cliff, and the rock selected for its site could be
levelled. The lighthouse is open on afternoons of fair weather and
the keepers always seem to appreciate visitors. This is the point
closest to Lundy, some twelve miles off shore and seen almost
end-on. The island has hitherto functioned as a break-water, and
from now on one experiences vastly different seas to the previous
stretch. To quote an anonymous poet,

> 'Where on Hartland's tempest-furrowed shore
> Breaks the long swell farthest Labrador.'

The swell is not the only thing to break along here. Back in
1852 William Hurton wrote in *Chamber's Journal*

Fragments of wreck everywhere attest the nature of the coast. If an
unfortunate vessel is driven by a north-west or a south-west gale within
the Horns of Hartland and Padstow Points, God help her hapless crew!
for she is doomed to certain destruction. Along the whole coast there is

no harbour of refuge — nothing but iron rocks. Here the roar of the ocean is incessant, and in stormy weather appalling. Mighty waves then fling themselves against the giant cliffs, and bursting with thundering crash, send their spray in salt-showers over the land. The life led by the dwellers near these solitary cliffs can be but dimly imagined by the inhabitants of inland cities. During the long dark nights of winter, they listen between the fierce bursts of the tempest, expecting every moment to hear the cry of human agony, from the crew of some foundering bark, rise above the wild laugh of the waves; and when morning breaks, they descend to the rugged beach, not knowing whether they may not find it strewn with wrecks and corpses. So tremendous is the power of the sea on this particular part of the coast, that masses of rock, from ten to twenty tons in weight, are frequently uplifted and hurled about the beach. Whatever stigma once attached to the people of the coast as wreckers who allured vessels to destruction or plundered and murdered the helpless crews cast ashore, a character the very reverse may most justly be claimed by the existing generation. Their conduct in all cases of shipwreck is admirable.

It is regrettable that the conduct of the local people in the case of the most recent wreck seems to have been less than admirable. The *Johanna*, a 978-ton Panamanian registered coaster, ran ashore just south of the lighthouse on the last day of 1982, and plundering her provided a holiday task for literally hundreds of 'wreckers'.

It also reveals uncertainty over the legal position laid down in the 1894 Merchant Shipping Act. The way it was interpreted in this case was that persons removing goods from the wreck and afterwards notifying the authorities were not committing an offence, which is quite rational where the ship is expected to break up on the next high tide. In fact the bulk of the goods were located, but it is difficult to believe that people came from all over the south-west to act as 'minders'.

The most impressive feature of the cliffs running southwards from here is the geological one, with the revelation of all the folds in the structural geology textbooks, and a few that aren't. The action of the sea in eroding away the weaker shales means that the sandstones remain prominently displayed, and the folds can be studied both in plan and elevation. One normally thinks of sandstone as a hard, brittle rock, and yet the evidence of one's eyes is that when subjected to immense pressures acting over a sufficiently long period it will bend, behaving like putty.

Explanations of what caused these pressures have changed over the years. In 1849 Kingsley wrote of the strata 'being pressed and squeezed together like reams of wet paper between the rival granite pincers of Dartmoor and Lundy.' But with the advent of radio-active dating it was revealed that the Lundy granite was a mere fifty million years old compared with the 250-300 million years of the other south-west granites, while the folding is believed to be slightly older than the oldest granites.

Today the young science of plate tectonics may provide a better explanation. This is one of very many subjects on which I am not an authority, and my belief is that it has yet to make an impact in explaining the structure of what geologists like to call the Cornubian province.

Only since the 1960s has it become accepted that the continents are not static but drift over the planet's surface, powered by the convection currents deep in the Earth's mantle. Collisions between adjacent continental plates can cause the surface rocks to ruck up like a carpet, while my understanding of more recent work is that it suggests that deeper down the pressures and temperatures are such that a chemical change can occur in the lower crust to give rise to molten granite. This being lighter can rise up to perhaps within a mile of the surface, where it crystallises. Where this has happened, erosion over the succeeding millions of years has stripped off the covering rocks to sufficient depth to reveal the granite tors which stretch at intervals from Dartmoor to Land's End.

The whole period of disturbance is termed the Variscan (or in older books Hercynian or even Armorican) Orogeny, or mountain building, the usual effect of prolonged plate collisions being to throw up mountain ranges. There is, incidentally, a link here with another of the World's great walks. Before the Atlantic Ocean began to open about a hundred million years ago, what was to become Britain abutted onto Eastern North America. There, the Variscan upheaval is known as the Appalachian Orogeny. This gave rise to that range of mountains now traversed by the Appalachian Trail, which I believe was the World's first Government-sponsored long-distance path.

To continue the walk, this follows fields above Blagdon Cliff before reaching the cliff edge at Upright Cliff, appropriately shear at one point, before descending to Titchberry Water. Here is the first example of a sea capture since the Valley of Rocks, and again a minority claims that it is an ice-marginal channel. In support of this view it is suggested that the valleys are more U-shaped than the expected V-shaped, the inference being that they were formed under glacial conditions.

A few hundred yards upstream from the over-elaborate bridge is the massive earth bank of what was a medieval fishpond, (surprisingly this seems not to have been owned by Hartland Abbey). Having gained the top of the cliff again, one then has to descend into the dry valley (actually it is rather boggy) below Smoothlands, the original course of Titchberry Water before the sea eroded into the valley by the present waterfall. The tiny stream remaining falls to the shore by Damehole Point, which is accessible by a right of way, although it would take someone with steadier nerves than mine to venture up the narrow ridge of scree.

Around here in May one encounters for the first time the spring squill, another very characteristic plant of the cliff-tops and virtually confined to north and west facing coasts. Occasionally it grows so profusely that it colours whole patches of the cliff a pale blue. The presence of bracts distinguishes it from the autumn squill, which is less well named, being at its best in August, and which is even more localised. Both are close relatives of the bluebell.

The slog up Blegberry Cliff follows. Half a mile inland is Blegberry Farm, which was fortified during the Civil War. Then comes the descent to Blegberry Water, overlooked by a modern house. Here the stream is crossed by what is almost a dam. Page refers to this spot as Black Mouth.

Berry Cliff has next to be gained, followed by the descent to Blackpool Mill, where the Abbey River runs into the sea. The river has been artifically straightened, the mill marking the site of one of the original meanders. Just over a mile upstream is Hartland Abbey, rebuilt in 1860, although the original foundation was eleventh century. The river is crossed by another over-elaborate bridge, after which the best views are vouchsafed to those who keep right to the edge of Dyer's lookout, said to have been named after a local miller.

The climb up to the Warren now follows, and then, mercifully, a level stretch for nearly half a mile. The prominent ruin ahead is known as the Pleasure House. Page is in no doubt as to its origin — 'built by an invalid once residing at the Abbey, who would visit it daily to drink in the sea breeze'. Prominent inland is the Abbey Church of St Nectan, the 'Cathedral of North Devon'. Another rocket post stands on the cliff, and the road is reached next to the rocket apparatus house, now converted into a cottage.

For those who want to visit the church, a public footpath runs for the half-mile just to the north of the roadside hedge. The official walk is continued by finding a path leading steeply down to Hartland Quay, which is on the valley floor of what was the Wargery Water until the sea broke through the valley wall 600 yards to the south. The actual quay must have been roughly contemporary with the pier at Clovelly, dating from about 1600. It ran north-west for nearly a hundred yards, the pierhead forming a right angle just short of Life Rock (so called because of the tradition that the sea never broke over it and hence anyone shipwrecked who managed to reach it would survive).

The existence of the quay meant that a small trading community was able to grow up over the years in this extremely exposed situation. However, when the railway reached Bideford in 1855 trade fell away and repairs were no longer economic. In 1887 a gale took away the pierhead, and the buildings along one side of the street were converted into a hotel. In 1896 another storm completed the work of destruction so comprehensively that even at low tide it is difficult to trace the course of the pier. In 1979 local volunteers completed work on a little slipway, to be used mostly by lobster fishermen. A small museum is open in the summer and illustrates very well the changes experienced here over the past 400 years.

To the south of the Quay, to quote Arber, 'the grandeur of the rocks laid bare in the cliffs by sea erosion, and of the reefs on the shore, almost defies description. It is, perhaps, the finest scenery in the whole stretch of this coast-line.'

Resuming the walk, one passes into a nature reserve set up with the intention of preserving the Large Blue butterfly. A hundred years ago it could be found as far away as Northamptonshire, but for reasons not fully understood it then began to decline, and it was around here that it made its last stand. Although one collection of 700 specimens was sold between the wars, over-collecting does not seem to have been the main cause. The caterpillars feed initially on the wild thyme growing among the close-cropped turf. They have a gland secreting a sugary substance attractive to one particular species of ant. The critical stage in the life history of the Large Blue depends on the ants carrying the caterpillars into their nests, where they feed on their larvae, and then hibernate and pupate. The butterfly emerges after ten months.

With the spread of myxomatosis and decline of nature's own lawn-mowers, the close-cropped turf was replaced by coarser grasses, making things difficult for both the thyme and the ants. Despite the establishment of a high-powered committee specifically to conserve the Large Blue, and the award of the MBE to a gentleman who bought a piece of land for the same end, it was officially declared extinct in 1979. Attempts are being made at a secret locality to re-introduce it from France.

Continuing south, the knife-edge of Screda Point projects prominently into the Atlantic, and after some hundred yards one passes below Bradstone's Well, the waters of which were supposed to cure sore eyes. The ultimate in fatuous folklore is surely reached a couple of hundred yards inland, where there is a standing stone which is said to turn itself around every time it hears the church bells ring.

After passing the waterfall of Wargery Water, with St Catherine's Tor behind it, 'a huge rounded hill cut in two by the encroaching ocean as by a giant's sword' as Tugwell described it, the path goes through a wooden gate between the stream and a massive bank, the lower half stone-faced. This was once the dam of a medieval swannery. On the tor there used to be a chapel to St Catherine. It is interesting to find, as at Abbotsbury, the association of a swannery with a hill-top chapel to that saint. Charles Kingsley, despite becoming Professor of History at Cambridge, was no antiquary. He interpreted the medieval tiles as being Roman and inferred that here was the site of a Roman villa.

The Wargery Water is crossed by concrete stepping stones, and despite the loss of the Large Blue, this area remains a good one for butterflies. I have found the Green Hairstreak and the Small Pearl-bordered and Dark Green fritillaries within a few hundred yards in late June.

A climb of 200 feet has then to be faced, from which one descends to Speke's Mill Mouth. According to Arber this was 'by far the grandest and most imposing series of falls on the whole coast. . . . Undoubtedly, when the existence of this fall becomes better known, it will be an object of pilgrimage.' He devoted six and a half pages to a description of it accompanied by five photographs.

Charles Kingsley's sister Charlotte was here fifty years before Arber, but was more concerned with the rural economy, as was her brother at Mouth Mill:

...far below you, dozens of donkeys looking like mice, being laden with sand on the beach. The path is narrow, rough, and steep, and you are obliged to keep out of the way of the donkeys with their wet sacks, as they toil up heavily laden, or are driven down pell mell (invariably choosing the best and safest part of the road) by wild little urchins who, at a certain corner, leave the animals to their own inventions, and, seating themselves on a large pebble, slide down the smooth face of a sloping rock, which is scored with the slides of preceding generations.

The actual sand was stored in bays still traceable by the bridge.

Once over the bridge, by keeping as close as practicable to the cliffs one passes above Brownspear Point, where tradition has it that 'Cruel Coppinger' was the sole survivor of a shipwreck in 1792. There certainly was a person of that surname; the Hartland parish register records the marriage in August 1793 of Daniel Herbert Copinger and Anne Hamlyn of Galsham. Galsham was a farm a mile and a half inland, but that is all that can be said with any certainty. Hawker wrote an account of Coppinger, giving free rein to his vivid imagination, with the result that no one will ever succeed in separating the fact from the fiction. He refers to 'a ballad in existence within human memory . . . of which the first verse only can now be recovered.'

'Will you hear of the Cruel Coppinger?
He came from a foreign kind:
He was brought to us by the salt water,
He was carried away by the wind.'

It is difficult to believe that such lawlessness as Hawker recounts could have survived into the last decade of the eighteenth century.

Resuming the walk up the significantly named Swansford Hill, the view on a clear day extends well beyond Tintagel, even, if conditions are exceptional, to Trevose Head thirty-five miles away. In 1895 Page wrote 'I doubt if there be any half-mile free from the debris of ships that have ended their last voyage on this iron-bound coast', and it is particularly true of this stretch. At low tide the wreckage of several unfortunate ships can still be glimpsed.

The most celebrated of recent years was the *Green Ranger*, a Royal Fleet Auxiliary which parted her tow in a gale in 1962. Rescue efforts involved the Appledore lifeboat, a helicopter from RAF Chivenor, and the Hartland lifesaving association, the last-named managing to save the crew of seven, by breeches buoy, just before the ship broke in two. Scrap from the wreck has been left lying around the cliff-top, near the Gunpath, which provides a suicidal descent of 400 feet to the beach.

Nearly half a mile further brings one to two new stiles, and a signpost indicating the presence of Hartland youth hostel, with its somewhat spartan comforts, half a mile inland. It was along the track to it that I had my closest encounter with a peregrine falcon. As I turned the corner between the hedge banks I disturbed one on the ground, which took off over my shoulder like a rocket.

Continuing along the cliff, on my last visit the next field had been ploughed right to the edge, which ninety-nine times out of a hundred is a confounded nuisance, if not actually illegal. The hundredth time is when it passes a mesolithic site, such as Elmscott Gutter, the little channel at the far end. Just by slowing my pace I was able to observe some ten flint flakes as well as a pebble-tool, which is just a bevelled cylindrical pebble, very characteristic of south-west mesolithic man, and virtually all that there was available for bashing things with until neolithic man arrived with his technique of polishing stone axes.

Just beyond, one is forced out onto the road for what seems an unnecessarily long half-mile to avoid Sandhole Cliff, where Coppinger is said to have had his principal cave. A mile to the south-east is Goldenpark, the farm where according to tradition he was received following his shipwreck.

After returning to the cliffs, a mile of gentle climbing brings one to Embury Beacon, probably an Iron Age promontory fort, although the promontory must have been eroded away over two thousand years. Erosion was proceeding at such a rapid rate that a rescue dig was mounted here in 1972-3. The low outer rampart has a trace of a ditch outside and is assumed to have protected a cattle enclosure. The more substantial inner rampart and ditch guarded the living area, evidenced only by postholes, hearths and pottery. The pottery had been made from gabbroic clay, found only around Coverack down on the Lizard, a resource first exploited in the early Neolithic period. What was marked on the maps as a tumulus for many years was revealed to be all that remained of the entrance to the settlement.

It used to be thought that the oldest defensive earthworks dated from the Iron Age, but recent excavations in Dorset and Gloucestershire have shown that they originated in the early Neolithic period. This evidence of man's aggressive nature from such an early stage in the archaeological record leads to the depressing inference that such aggression is innate behaviour.

A level half-mile brings one to Knap Head, after which one starts to descend to the Strawberry Water, with initially a view of Welcombe Church, a mile inland. Parson Hawker, vicar of Morwenstow, took over the incumbency of the parish of Welcombe in 1850 in an attempt to relieve his pressing financial problems.

At the bottom one arrives at Welcombe Mouth, one of very few places along this stretch that are accessible to the motorist. Once over the concrete stepping stones Hartland parish is finally left behind. According to George Tugwell's *North Devon Handbook* dated 1856, the last case of deliberate wrecking occurred in Welcombe parish 'about five years ago', but no evidence was quoted, and it is difficult to see Hawker remaining silent in such circumstances.

At low tide there is an alternative route along the shore, over the sharp reefs of slippery seaweed covered rock, but almost certainly it provides for slower progress than 'over the top'. However, it does allow the geologically inclined to get a better view of Variscan folding. I particularly favour the official route in September, because despite the exposed situation, the blackberries that border the path grow as large and and sweet as anywhere else I can remember.

At the summit the fence is composed of railway sleepers, which, as Philip Carter observed, must have come a long way. Even before the Beeching Axe, Hartland used to advertise itself as 'Farthest from Railways'. Half a mile inland is Mead Farm, the home until his death in 1982 of the unconventional poet and playwright Ronald Duncan. Its proximity to certain defence installations led to his constructing a nuclear fall-out shelter, albeit one without any ventilation. On the way down one passes his little hut, for which the local council refused planning permission, but he appealed successfully. It is now an artist's studio.

And so one comes to the little footbridge over the Marsland Water, that marks the boundary between Devon and Cornwall, a quite isolated spot in utter contrast to the mouth of the other river dividing the two counties. The geomorphologist will note that above the gorge are terraces cut in the head at both the fifty foot and hundred foot contours. The mill was restored by Ronald Duncan just before the last war.

In his *Westward Ho!* Charles Kingsley has described this area superbly.

...those delightful glens, which cut the high table-land of the confines of Devon and Cornwall, and opening each through its gorge of down and rock, towards the boundless Western Ocean. Each is like the other, and each is like no other English scenery. Each has its upright walls, inland of rich oak-wood, nearer the sea of dark green furze, then of smooth turf, then of weird black cliffs which range out right and left far into the deep sea, in castles, spires, and wings of jagged iron-stone. Each has its narrow strip of fertile meadow, its crystal trout stream winding across and across from one hill-foot to the other; its grey stone mill, with the water sparkling and humming round the dripping wheel; its dark rock pools above the tide mark, where the salmon-trout gather in from their Atlantic wanderings, after each Autumn flood; its ridge of blown sand, bright with golden trefoil and crimson lady's finger; its grey bank of polished pebbles, down which the stream rattles toward the sea below. Each has its black field of jagged shark's-tooth rock which paves the cove from side to side, streaked with here and there a pink line of shell sand, and laced with white foam from the eternal surge, stretching in parallel lines out to the westward, in strata set upright on edge, or tilted towards each other at strange angles by primeval earthquakes; — such is the 'Mouth' — as those coves are called; and such the jaw of teeth which they display, one rasp of which would grind abroad the timbers of the stoutest ship. To landward, all richness, softness, and peace; to seaward, a waste and howling wilderness of rock and roller, barren to the fisherman, and hopeless to the shipwrecked mariner. In only one of these Mouths is a landing for boats, made possible by a long sea-wall of rock, which protects it from the rollers of the Atlantic; and that mouth is Marsland.

My own guess is that very few boats have landed at such an isolated spot since Kingsley's day.

Once across the stream one is in the parish of Morwenstow, indelibly linked with the name of Robert Stephen Hawker. In 1834 Bishop Philpotts had reservations about offering so isolated a parish to someone as gifted as Hawker, but the parish was to become his life for the next forty years.

My seaward boundary was a stretch of bold and rocky shore, an interchange of lofty headland and deep and sudden gorge, the cliff varying from three hundred to four hundred and fifty feet of perpendicular or gradual height, and the valleys gushing with torrents, which bounded rejoicingly towards the sea, and leaped at last, amid a cloud of spray, into the waters. So stern and pitiless is this iron bound coast, that within the memory of one man upwards of eighty wrecks have been counted within a reach of fifteen miles, with only here and there the rescue of a living man. My people were a mixed multitude of smugglers, wreckers, and dissenters of various hues.

He went on to explain that he used the word wrecker to mean 'a watcher of the sea and rocks for flotsam and jetsam, and other unconsidered trifles which the waves might turn up to reward the zeal and vigilance of a patient man.'

The climb out of Marsland Mouth is relatively easy, but once past Gull Rock a 'deep and sudden gorge' has to be negotiated, dropping down to the seventy foot waterfall of Litter Mouth. The stream is crossed, as are most streams in this parish, by a bridge fashioned very economically from two telegraph poles. Then follows the slog up to 400 feet at Cornakey Cliff before dropping down to about 150 feet to cross the Yeol Water. The switchback is continued with a climb up to the 450 feet summit of Henna Cliff, said to be the highest sheer drop on the South West Way, and with a more extensive view than the previous few. For the first time the dish aerials at Cleave are visible, while across the combe are Morwenstow Church, and the Rectory built by Hawker in 1837 with its chimneys said to resemble the towers of churches with which he had been associated.

A descent of 300 feet brings one down to the waterfall of the Morwenstow Water. The path down to the beach and Hawker's bathing pool has long since eroded away, as has St Morwenna's Well, which was near the cliff edge some hundred yards to the south. An illustration of it accompanied an article Hawker wrote for the *Gentleman's Magazine* in 1867.

Having gained the summit of Vicarage Cliff it is very well worth while making a diversion inland for 600 yards to look around the churchyard. To quote from Hawker's 1867 article:

Along and beneath the southern trees, side by side, are the graves of between thirty and forty seamen, hurled by the sea, in shipwreck, on the neighbouring rocks, and gathered up and buried there by the present vicar and his people. The crews of three lost vessels, cast away upon the rocks of the glebe and elsewhere, are laid at rest in this safe and silent ground. A legend for one recording-stone thus commemorates a singular scene. The figure-head of the brig *Caledonia*, of Arbroath, in Scotland, stands at the graves of her crew, in the churchyard of Morwenstow:

> We laid them in their lowly rest,
> The strangers of a distant shore: —
> We smoothed the green turf on their breast,
> 'Mid baffled ocean's angry roar!
> And there — the relique of the storm —
> We fixed fair Scotland's figured form.

The figure-head, although of wood, remains remarkably well-preserved after 140 years. The following year nine of the crew of the Stockton schooner *Alonzo* were buried, the grave being marked by a boat, keel uppermost, and a pair of oars crosswise, but these have not survived. It was this action that led an Exeter newspaper, the High Church *Flindell's Western Luminary* to comment:

Strangers as they were, receiving their last resting place from the charity of the inhabitants upon whose coast they were thrown, they have not been piled one upon another, in a common pit, but are buried side by side, each in his own grave. This may seem a trifle; but reverence for the remains of the departed is a Christian virtue, and is associated with the most sublime and consolatory doctrine of our holy religion. They who thus honour the dead, will seldom fail in their duty to the living.

Some of Hawker's accounts are as harrowing as anything to be met with along the path. The razor-sharp rocks meant that too often it was merely pieces of body that were found, perhaps up to a month after the wreck. Even then the remains could not be buried until the coroner had arrived, 'and the usual verdict of "Wrecked and cast ashore" empowered me to inter the dead sailors.' Before the passing of the Seaman's Burial Act in 1808 'it was the common usage of the coast to dig, just above high water mark, a pit on the shore, and therein to cast, without inquest or religious rite, the carcases of shipwrecked men.' Hawker would personally double the five shillings reward that the Act prescribed for notifying the finding of a corpse.

Although the subject of several biographies of increasing merit, Hawker himself remains an enigmatic figure. In particular, his standing with his parishioners in an area where both the Wesleyans and the Bible Christians were particularly strong, is by no means clear. Baring-Gould has quoted a letter written by Hawker in 1850 that seems almost paranoid: 'Fifteen years I have been vicar of this altar, and all that while no lay person, landlord, tenant, parishioner, or steward, has ever proferred me even one kind word, much less aid or coin. Nay, I have found them all bristling with dislike.'

Not only is this difficult to reconcile with the 'amiable and gifted vicar' of Hurton's 1852 account, but it is now known that Hawker's extravagant tastes were financed by borrowing heavily from several Methodist parishioners. Many of his prose writings were intended to pay off debts, and have to be regarded as pot-boilers rather than as accurate accounts of his experiences. Indeed, his son-in-law C. E. Byles, who wrote the most detailed biography, accepted that Hawker was unable to distinguish fact and fancy.

One account of Hawker's preaching that has survived is from a visitor on a hot summer's day, who observed the congregation to consist of a few farmers and children, all asleep, while a sheep rubbed itself against the font. Yet it was Hawker who orginated the modern harvest festival service.

No one can doubt that Hawker was a man of genuinely creative talent, but the effect of forty years exile from fellow writers coupled with lack of the recognition that he deserved was to increase his original eccentricity and mysticism to the point where his rationality could be questioned. He was convinced that All Soul's Library preserved a document containing the authentic signature of the Devil, while his intolerance of dissenters went beyond the bounds of what was reasonable.

Following his controversial death-bed conversion to Roman Catholicism he was buried in Plymouth cemetery. On his memorial is carved appropriately a quotation from 'The Quest of the Sangraal', his most ambitious work, 'I would not be forgotten in this land.' Today, more than a hundred years after his death it is still not possible to think of Morwenstow without also thinking of Hawker.

The church is substantially Norman, built of stone from the cliffs, and seems on a generous scale for such a sparsely populated parish. An extremely detailed guidebook is available, and gives the full dedication as being to St Morwenna and St John the Baptist. Tradition has it that Morwenna was one of the twenty-four children of the Welsh King Brychan.

Cornish saint-lore remains a confusing blend of the possible, the improbable, and the impossible; but the traditions are of some value for the light they shed on the beliefs of earlier days. The early Christian period is currently fashionable among archaeologists and historians, and no doubt the combination of the two disciplines will eventually succeed in making the Dark Ages less dark.

On a more material note, just above the churchyard is the seasonal Rectory tea room, while a few hundred yards up the lane, facing the green, is the Bush Inn, stone floored and substantially unimproved — another pub which I am able to recommend.

Returning to the cliffs, 200 yards brings one to Hawker's Hut, set into the top of the 400 foot cliff, and originally fashioned by him from wreck-wood; it is now preserved by the National Trust. It was here that he would sit seeking inspiration for his writings and sermons, and here he was visited by Tennyson in 1848 and Charles Kingsley in 1849.

One soon drops down to the Tidna water, from where a diversion can be made to the waterfall, which Arber regarded as 'most curious'. From the little footbridge, the best route is to climb steeply up to the wartime breeze-block look-out, from where the sure-footed can make their way along what is almost an arête out to Higher Sharpnose Point, a very good viewpoint which dominates the view from the south for many miles.

Continuing south, after half a mile the larger-scale maps mark 'Oldwalls' by a very minor promontory, again hinting at some lost archaeological feature, conceivably another eroded cliff castle. A further half-mile takes one past the gently sloping point above Hippa Rock to the descent to Stanbury Mouth where an awkward little ravine has to be crossed. Those with time to spare and determination can scramble down the steep and stony path to the bench, which is sandy at low tide.

From here one has to slog back up to the 400 foot contour with pillboxes over to the left, erected to guard what became in the last war RAF Cleave. It survived as an anti-aircraft gunnery training unit until 1960, and subsequently with its four huge dish aerials became a top secret Composite Signals Organisation Station, an outpost of the controversial Government Communications Head-quarters at Cheltenham. Its main function is to monitor Soviet satellites, and it is said to make this area the fifth primary target on the Kremlin hit-list, so this is no place to be if the international situation should take a turn for the worse.

There are some who claim that CSOS Morwenstow has an

even more sinister function — they insist that it is run jointly with the US National Security Agency (which is bigger but more reticent than the CIA) and has been positioned here to monitor all telephone calls beamed to and from Goonhilly Downs Earth Station. The calls are said to be passed through a computer, and if certain key words are used the call is automatically recorded. It should not be necessary to add that such an intrusion into the privacy of the individual has never been sanctioned by Parliament.

I can pretend to no specialist knowledge of such matters, but I do know of someone, who, in the course of a casual visit to another communications establishment not ten miles away, was allowed to eavesdrop on a conversation between two American businessmen.

Spying seems to be a growth industry these days. The four aerials are shortly to be increased to seven. Not only are they ethically intrusive, but they are also visually intrusive, which prompted the local council to request that they be painted a more harmonious colour. The request was politely turned down.

Most walkers will be only too glad to turn their backs on it all, as they pass above Lower Sharpnose Point, where the cliffs are the resort of rock-climbers who must have nerves of steel. There is more than enough evidence of erosion around, particularly at Harscott High Cliff, where the fissures indicate that rotational slipping is in prospect. Two more pillboxes are visible to the left before one arrives at Steeple Point, overlooking Duckpool at the mouth of the Coombe Valley.

The name Duckpool is alleged to derive from its being the place where local witches were ducked. The name of Steeple Point used to puzzle me, with only the tower of Kilkhampton Church visible, until I learned that the original meaning of the word included a tower. Just to the left of the church is the Norman Motte and Bailey, given to the National Trust in 1973.

The Vicar of Kilkhampton from 1908 until 1940 wrote a history of the Parish and Church in which he complained that few of the original documents had survived. His successor, being of a more inquisitive nature, happened to open a box in the corner of the church and found it full of the missing records!

Half a mile inland is the hamlet of Coombe, which has associations with Hawker. It was at a cottage there, while on vacation from Oxford, that he elaborated a few lines of a traditional ballad into 'The Song of the Western Men', which, for some reason quite out of character, he published anonymously in a Plymouth newspaper. It was an instant success, but was not surprisingly assumed to be traditional, even by Sir Walter Scott and Lord Macaulay.

Hawker was later to complain '. . . all these years the song has been bought and sold, set to music and applauded, while I have lived on among these far away rocks unprofited, unpraised and unknown. This is an epitome of my whole life.' And also, with far less justification, 'Legends which from meagreness of the materials I almost entirely invented, I have recognised worked up and used as their own by Wilkie Collins, Walter White, and local thieves in troops.'

The other association concerns King William's Bridge at Coombe. The stream is normally little problem, but heavy rain causes it to rise very rapidly, and several of Hawker's parishioners were drowned trying to ford it. One of Hawker's first acts was to write to the Monarch, requesting that he support a public subscription for building a bridge. The King obliged with twenty pounds, but in fact the bulk of the money came from Hawker's first wife. The bridge was opened in 1837.

However, there was no path whatsoever along the southern side of the stream, so that coast-walkers heading north when it was in spate had to choose between turning back or risking the turbulent waters. Requests for a bridge here from the South West Way Association were initially refused, and it was not until 1981, eight years after the official opening ceremony, that the stony-hearted officials gave way.

For the geologically inclined, Duckpool is at the axis of the east-west running syncline that is the main structural feature of Devon. As one proceeds south one can expect to encounter progressively older rocks until the next major anticline near Mawgan Porth, although the picture is inevitably complicated by the faulting around Tintagel. The tightness of the folds, which measures the intensity of the deformation, is also said to increase as one proceeds south, although I cannot personally say that I have noticed.

Continuing the walk, one has to climb up to Warren Point, and this is quickly followed by the climb out of Warren Gutter. From there easier gradients prevail as far as Bude. Menachurch Point is prominent ahead as one drops down to Sandy Mouth, where the National Trust have a seasonal tea room. Regrettably, the tarmac car park destroyed one of only two sites in England of the perennial centaury.

> From here there is at low tide an alternative way along the sands, much the better route for the structural geologist. There are two escape routes if the tide has been misjudged, the first after a mile at Northcott Mouth, just beyond Menachurch Point, where there are the scanty remains of a First World War wreck, and half a mile further at Earthquake. The final half-mile seems to be the first to be covered by the returning tide. Those walking northward can get some indication of its state from the little half tide cross, which was placed on Coach Rock at Summerleaze Beach in 1846 by a relative of Sir Thomas Acland, the principal landowner.

The last time I took the cliff path from Sandy Mouth there was some ragged robin growing by a damp patch. A few years ago this would not have been worth a mention, but the plant is so sensitive to the effects of chemical sprays that it is now quite a rarity. After half a mile one passes old rifle range butts, and just before Menachurch Point there is a prominent round barrow. The hotels of Bude should now be visible ahead, as well as the spire of Flexbury Church and the tower of Poughill Church, almost hidden by trees.

The path now descends to Northcott Mouth, still disfigured by 1940 concrete tank traps. Beyond, erosion has forced a diversion behind a bungalow. Another 500 yards brings one to Earthquake, which is what rock-falls were sometimes called, particularly those that occurred just after the disastrous Lisbon earthquake of 1755.

Half a mile onward from here brings one to Crooklets Beach and the chance, in season, of a meal and a pint. The beach was dubbed the 'Second Bondi' by two Australian airmen during the last war. This led to the formation of Britain's first surf lifesaving club at Bude in 1953.

A further half-mile brings one past the cricket ground to a topograph and flag-staff (once the mast of the *Elizabeth*, a Salcombe-built ketch wrecked here in 1912) and into Bude, a quiet spacious resort. Finding accommodation should be no problem, but those anxious to continue the walk can, at low tide, cross the mouth of the little River Neet and the Bude canal lock.

This was Britain's most ambitious tub-boat canal, engineered by James Green, the barges being fitted with wheels to enable them to be hauled up inclined planes powered by water. One branch reached beyond Holsworthy and the other almost to Launceston. It was opened in 1823 primarily to carry sea-sand to inland farms, but it also carried coal and farm produce. Although an engineering success it was never a financial one, and its final demise came with the arrival of the railway in 1898.

The original breakwater was also built in 1823, but was destroyed in a storm fifteen years later, and was replaced with the present lower-profiled structure. The original name of Bude Haven is perhaps something of an exaggeration. The canal basin was accessible only for a couple of hours around high water, and even then not at neap tides. The channel is only some hundred yards wide, and in days of sail ran perilously close to Barrel and Chapel Rocks. The normal method of entry was for 'hobblers' to row out and take a rope from the vessel, enabling it to be warped into the lock. The word is presumably a local variant of 'hoveller', which most dictionaries give as meaning an uncertificated pilot.

At the peak of the coastal trade during the middle of the last century there were some fifty vessels owned locally. Those from other ports rarely ventured in, because they could be stuck there for up to a month before conditions allowed them out. It has been calculated that one in five of the local vessels were lost entering or leaving the port. Although there was a lifeboat from 1837 until 1923 the times when it could get out through the surf were minimal. An inshore rescue boat has since been located here.

There is a very good little museum in what used to be the blacksmith's shop by the canal basin. Among the items preserved is the figurehead from the *Bencoolen*, Bude's most controversial wreck, the full story of which will now never be known. Originally, the figurehead was erected over the twenty-six graves in the churchyard.

The *Bencoolen* was bound from Liverpool for Bengal with a general cargo in October 1862 when she was dismasted in a sudden gale in St George's Channel. She was driven before north-westerly winds for three days until she struck broadside on across Bude's entrance channel. The coastguard assembled their rocket apparatus on the breakwater, but were provided with only two rocket lines, both of which were carried away by heavy seas. Although most of the lifeboat crew were away, a reserve crew was found which set out, but was forced to turn back amid the jeers of spectators. Having realised their plight, the *Bencoolen* crew constructed a raft and as the ship broke in two they launched it into the pounding surf. Only six reached the shore alive.

At the resulting inquest all six survivors gave evidence under oath that when disaster struck the Captain had locked himself in his cabin and taken to drink. One even claimed that 'the Captain was not thoroughly sober from the time we left Liverpool, and was so drunk as to be incapable of taking charge of the ship from the time of her being dismasted.' The jury returned a verdict of accidental death, with a recommendation to the Board of Trade that in future a better supply of line be provided for the use of the rocket apparatus.

But that was not the end of the story. A few days after the inquest three of the survivors appeared before a Commissioner for Oaths and gave a radically revised version, swearing that the loss of the ship was not through the neglect or default of the master, who had done his duty to the utmost of his power. In addition, the owner of the ship, Edward Bates, wrote an angry letter to the Liverpool *Morning Herald*, claiming that its report of the wreck was biased and asking for an apology.

The problem is to know who to believe. Hawker was in no doubt that 'there was some vile atrocity commited among that crew ... the gold watch of the Captain [was found] in the steward's pocket.' But I have discovered no contemporary report to substantiate Baring-Gould's version that the survivors were too drunk to attend the funeral of their colleagues.

Hawker's scorn for the lifeboat crew gave rise to his bitter 'A

Croon on Hennacliff':

> ' "Cawk! cawk!" then said the raven,
> "I am fourscore years and ten;
> Yet never in Bude Haven
> Did I croak for rescued men." '

The lifeboat crew were exonerated after an official inquiry. The following year, when the *Margaret Quayle* was in difficulties a few miles up the coast, at a time when the Chief Inspector of Lifeboats, Captain Ward, was making his annual inspection, he took over the command of the lifeboat; but as soon as she was clear of the breakwater ordered her back.

A little-known sequel to the *Bencoolen* wreck began in 1871, with the election of Edward Bates as the Conservative MP for Plymouth, while his enemies claimed that he was too well known around Liverpool to have had any chance of being elected nearer home. His parliamentary career was not uneventful.

The Parliament also contained Mr Samuel Plimsoll, representing Derby in the Liberal interest, who in the following year published a book entitled *Our Seamen*, which contained irrefutable proof that the lives of seamen were being sacrificed to enhance the profits of shipowners. It also contained the sentence 'Nevertheless, owing to the fact that two or three of what they call in the North "The greatest sinners in the Trade", having got into the House, it is there, and only there, that opposition to reform is to be expected, or is found.' This was probably not aimed at Bates because the Members for Tynemouth, Hull and Sunderland took it as a personal affront and complained to the Speaker, who ruled that it constituted a Breach of Privilege, for which Mr Plimsoll was forced to apologise.

Both Plimsoll's parents were born in Plymouth, so he had reason to interest himself in its representation, and on July 22nd 1875 he turned his attention to Bates. To quote from the usually arid pages of *Hansard*:

Mr PLIMSOLL: Then, Sir, I give Notice that on Tuesday next I will put this Question to the right hon. Gentlemen the President of the Board of Trade. I will ask the right hon. Gentleman whether he will inform the House as to the following ships — the *Tethys*, the *Melbourne*, the *Nora Greame*, which were all lost in 1874 with 87 lives, and the *Foundling* and *Sydney Dacres*, abandoned in the early part of this year, representing in all a tonnage of 9,000 tons and I shall ask whether the registered owner of these ships, Edward Bates, is the Member for Plymouth, or if it is some other person of the same name. ('Order!') And, Sir, I shall ask some questions about Members on this side of the House also. I am determined to unmask the villains who send to death and destruction − − (Loud cries of 'Order!' and much excitement)

Mr SPEAKER: The hon. Members makes use of the word 'villains'. I presume that the hon. Gentleman does not apply that expresison to any Member of this House.

Mr PLIMSOLL: I beg pardon?

Mr SPEAKER: The hon. Member made use of the word 'villains'. I trust he did not use it with reference to any Member of this House.

Mr PLIMSOLL: I did, Sir, and I do not mean to withdraw it. (Loud cries of 'Order!')

Mr SPEAKER: The expression of the hon. Member is altogether un-Parliamentary, and I must again ask him whether he persists in using it.

Mr PLIMSOLL: And I must again decline to retract ('Order!')

Mr SPEAKER: Does the hon. Member withdraw the expression?

Mr PLIMSOLL: No, I do not.

Mr SPEAKER: I must again call upon the hon. Member to withdraw the expression.

Mr PLIMSOLL: I will not.

Mr SPEAKER: If the hon. Gentleman does not withdraw the expression I must submit his conduct to the judgement of the House.

Mr PLIMSOLL: I shall be happy to submit to the judgement of the House ...

Following this 'unparalleled conduct' Mr Plimsoll was forced once again to apologise to the House, which knowing that he had the backing of the country, was forced to accept, although Mr Bates never received the personal apology to which he felt entitled.

Bates was further embroiled in controversy the following year when one of his ships docked at Falmouth with the crew suffering from scurvy, but this did not prevent his re-election in April 1880 (when Disraeli's Government was decisively rejected), to be rewarded with a baronetcy in the dissolution honours.

The Plymouth Liberals, however, petitioned against his return, alleging corrupt practices. At the ensuing inquiry it was revealed that Sir Edward had been in the habit of distributing blankets and coal among the poorer electors. The two judges seemed to regard this as a praiseworthy example of genuine benevolence, but they were forced to draw the line at the action of his agent, who had travelled down to Penzance and paid some Plymouth fishermen their rail fares to come home to vote, as well as for their time away from their boats. Sir Edward was declared not duly elected, but having found the case against him proven, the judges went on to criticise the Liberals for bringing it, apparently on the grounds that his loss would deprive the deserving poor of their winter comforts. It was left to the radical *Western Times* to point out that if a shipowner had any charitable instincts they were better directed to the widows and orphans of sailors from the 570 ships lost with all hands over the previous five years.

Inspite of all this, Sir Edward was re-elected in 1885 and represented Plymouth until he retired in 1892. He died four years later on his extensive Hampshire estate, 'a capable and successful businessman' according to his obituary in *The Times*.

From the public transport point-of-view Bude provides the best point to break off the walk until Padstow is reached, since there are four buses to Exeter on a weekday, and one on Sundays, provided by Jennings Ltd. For those fortunate enough to continue the walk there is much of interest ahead.

LIST OF SOURCES

Acts of Parliament

1609   7 James I, c.18
1736   9 George II, c.35, s.18

Official Publications

Special Instructions for the Coast Guard of the United Kingdom. 1866
Report of the Committee on Land Utilisation in Rural Areas. Cmnd 6378.
     1942
National Parks in England and Wales. Cmnd 6628. 1945
Report of the National Parks Committee. Cmnd 7121. 1947
Footpaths and Access to the Countryside. Cmnd 7207. 1947
A Study of Exmoor: Report by Lord Porchester. 1977
Hansard. 1875, 1910, 1946, 1949.

Law Reports

Chancery Reports. 1891, 1905
Justice of the Peace and Local Government Review. 1925

Authors

Adams, J. H. 'New Light on R. S. Hawker' in the *Cornish Review.*
     Autumn 1967
Arber, E. A. N. *The Coast Scenery of North Devon.* 1911
Ayton, Richard. *A Voyage Round Great Britain.* 1814
Baring-Gould, Sabine. *The Vicar of Morwenstow.* 1876
Beresford, G. C. *Schooldays with Kipling.* 1936
Black's Guide to Devonshire. 1911 ed.
Boyle, Vernon C. *Devon Harbours.* 1952
Browning, Robert. *A History of Golf.* 1955
Byles, C. E. *Life and Letters of R. S. Hawker.* 1905
Chadwyck-Healey, Sir Charles. *A History of Part of West Somerset.* 1901
Chanter, Charlotte. *Ferny Combes.* 1856
Chanter, J. M. *Wanderings in North Devon.* 1887

Chanter, J. R. 'History and Antiquities' in the *North Devon Handbook*. 1877 ed.

Coles, W. Crosbie. *Kingsley's Country*. 1894

Collinson, John. *The History and Antiquities of the County of Somerset*. 1791

Cooper, T. H. *Guide Containing a Short Historical Sketch of Lynton, Lynmouth, Ilfracombe, etc*. 1853

Cross, J. W. *George Eliot's Life*. vol I. 1885

Davidson, James. *Notes on the Antiquities of Devonshire*. 1861

Dawson, E. C. *James Hannington*. 1887

Defoe, Daniel. *A Tour Through the Whole Island of Britain*. 1724-6. Everyman edition, 1927

Dunsterville, Maj.-Gen. L. G. *Stalky's Reminiscences*. 1928

Lord Eversley. *Commons, Forests and Footpaths*. 1910

Gilpin, William. *Observations on the Mountains and Lakes of Cumberland and Westmorland*. 1772

Gosse, P. H. *A Naturalist's Rambles on the Devonshire Coast*. 1853
Seaside Pleasures. 1856

Hawker, R. S. *Cornish Ballads*. 1869
Footprints of Former Men in Far Cornwall. 1870

Hazlitt, William. 'My First Acquaintance with Poets' in *Uncollected Essays*. 1933

Johns, C. A. *Flowers of the Field*. 1st ed. 1851

Kingsley, Charles. 'North Devon' in *Fraser's Magazine*. 1849, reprinted in *Prose Idylls*. 1873
Westward Ho! 1855
Presidential Address in *Transactions of the Devonshire Association*, 1871
Poems. 1872

Kipling, Rudyard. *Stalky & Co*. 1899

Leland, John. *Itinerary*. ed. Lucy Toulmin Smith, 1907

Murray's Handbook to Devon and Cornwall. 1st ed. 1850

Nicholls, J. F. *Guide to Lynton and Lynmouth*. 1874

Norway, Arthur H. *Highways and Byways in Devon and Cornwall*. 1897

Osborn, Betty. *Parish Surveys in Somerset 5: Minehead Without*. 1983

Page, J. L. W. *An Exploration of Exmoor*. 1890
The Coasts of Devon and Lundy Island. 1895
The North Coast of Cornwall. 1897

Plimsoll, Samuel. *Our Seamen*. 1872

Pollock, Sir Frederick. 'Herring Counting' in *Notes and Queries*. 1874

The Land Laws. 3rd ed. 1896

Polwhele, Richard. *Historical Views of Devonshire.* 1793
    History of Devonshire. 1793-1806

Rawnsley, H. D. 'Footpath Preservation' in *Contemporary Review*, 1886

Risdon, Tristram. *The Chorographical Description or Survey of the County
    of Devon.* 1st ed. 1714

Shore, Henry N. *Smuggling Days and Smuggling Ways.* 1892

Southey, Robert. *Common-Place Book* vol 4. 1799

Stephen, Sir Leslie. 'Stray Thoughts on Scenery' in the *Cornhill
    Magazine.* 1878
    'In Praise of Walking' in *Monthly Review.* 1901

Thornton, W. H. *Reminiscences and Reflections of an Old Westcountry
    Clergyman.* 1897

Trevelyan, G. M. 'Walking' in *Clio, a Muse.* 1913

Tugwell, George. *North Devon Handbook.* 1856 and 1877 eds.
    North Devon Scenery Book. 1863

Ward, C. S. *Thorough Guide to North Devon and North Cornwall.*
    8th ed. 1903

Warner, Richard. *A Walk Through some of the Western Counties of
    England.* 1799
    A Tour Through Cornwall, in the Autumn of 1808. 1809

White, Walter. *A Londoner's Walk to the Land's End.* 1855
    A Month in Yorkshire. 1861

Woodward, H. B. *The History of the Geological Society of London.* 1907

Wordsworth, Dorothy. *The Letters of William and Dorothy Wordsworth.*
    vol. I. 1967

Newspapers and Periodicals

Chamber's Edinburgh Journal, 1852

The *Cornishman*, 1905

Flindell's Western Luminary, 1843

The Gentleman's Magazine, 1867

Ilfracombe *Parish Magazine*, 1904

John Bull, 1868

The *North Devon Journal*, various dates

The *Observer*, 1928

The *Pall Mall Gazette*, 1883, 1885

The *Royal Cornwall Gazette*, 1862

South West Way Association *Newsletters*, 1973–84
The Times, various dates
Trewman's Exeter Flying Post, various dates
United Services Journal, 1839
The *Western Morning News*, various dates
The *Western Times*, 1841, 1880
Woolmer's Exeter and Plymouth Gazette, 1835, 1876

Archive Material

Westcountry Studies Library, Exeter
Prespectus of the Northam Burrows Hotel and Villas Co. 1863
North Devon Athenaeum, Barnstaple
Report of the Admiralty Survey of the Taw Estuary of 1832, carried
out by Capt. H. M. Denham, RN, FRS, 1847

INDEX